ALEXANDER THE GREAT

SON OF THE GODS

ALEXANDER THE GREAT

SON OF THE GODS

ALAN FILDES
JOANN FLETCHER

AN INTIMATE PORTRAIT OF THE WORLD'S GREATEST CONQUEROR

DUNCAN BAIRD PUBLISHERS
LONDON

Alexander the Great: Son of the Gods
Alan Fildes and Joann Fletcher

First published in the United Kingdom and Ireland in 2001 by
Duncan Baird Publishers Ltd
Sixth Floor
Castle House
75–76 Wells Street
London W1T 3QH

Conceived, created and designed by Duncan Baird Publishers

Managing Editor: Diana Loxley
Editor: Joanne Clay
Designers: Paul Reid and Lloyd Tilbury at Cobalt id
Picture Researcher: Cee Weston-Baker
Commissioned artwork: Sally Taylor and Peter Visscher
Decorative borders: Sally Taylor
Commissioned maps: Neil Gower

British Library Cataloguing-in-Publication Data:
A CIP record for this book is available from the British Library.

ISBN: 1-903296-21-8

10 9 8 7 6 5 4 3 2 1

Typeset in Caslon 10.5/16pt
Colour reproduction by Colourscan, Singapore
Printed in Hong Kong by Imago

NOTE
The abbreviations CE and BCE are used throughout this book:
CE Common Era (the equivalent of AD)
BCE Before the Common Era (the equivalent of BC)

HALF-TITLE PAGE:
A Roman bronze statuette of Alexander astride Bucephalas.
FRONTISPIECE:
Detail of a Roman marble bust of Alexander—a copy of a Greek
original dated 338BCE.

CONTENTS

INTRODUCTION

Alexander the Great is one of the most celebrated figures of classical antiquity. In his relatively short reign (336–323BCE), the Macedonian king—portrayed here in a late 2nd-century BCE sculpture found at Magnesia—became the ruler of many nations, the world's wealthiest man, and was ultimately worshiped as a god. *Alexander the Great: Son of the Gods* explores the extraordinary career of this mighty conqueror, and also focuses on areas of his life that are often neglected, such as the key role played by his mother Olympias and the far-reaching effects of his time in Egypt.

Born in a remote kingdom in northern Greece as one of several royal sons, Alexander displayed leadership abilities at an early age and carved out a role for himself as heir to the Macedonian throne. Following the death of his father, Philip II, Alexander III secured the whole of Greece and prepared to lead its allied states against the massive Persian empire. He marched his army into Asia in 334BCE and fought his way against overwhelming odds through Asia Minor, Syria, and on to Egypt. The king then turned east into the Persian heartlands, where, at the age of 25, without incurring a single defeat, he became Great King of Persia by right of conquest.

Alexander—king, politician, scholar, and explorer—was above all a soldier. An acknowledged military genius, he was genuinely loved by his troops. Nevertheless, his belief in his own indestructibility meant he could be reckless, not only with his own life but also with the lives of his men, whom he expected to follow him on his often hazardous exploits across the known world. Their long campaigns left an indelible imprint on the landscapes and cultures of Asia and the East. Everywhere he went, Alexander founded Greek cities. By the time he died, he ruled over the greatest empire the world has ever seen—an empire composed of millions of ethnically diverse peoples who were united by a common Greek tongue.

In the two millennia since his death, the young conqueror has been portrayed in countless ways—from Alexander the Great to Iskander the Accursed, chivalrous knight to bloody monster, cultured scholar to drunken sadist, benign multi-culturalist to racist imperialist, pious celibate to sexual predator. Alexander's belief in his own divinity—one of the most puzzling aspects of his personality for modern observers—must be seen in the context of an ancient world in which the line between mortal and divine was at best blurred.

We have drawn heavily on Arrian and Plutarch as the most reliable of all the ancient sources in our attempts to discover the historical Alexander. *The Campaigns of Alexander* (*Anabasis Alexandri*), written by Arrian of Nicomedeia (Asia Minor) ca. 150CE, is based on the eyewitness accounts of two men who knew Alexander intimately. The first account was written by Alexander's friend, general, and rumored half-brother Ptolemy, whose account of the king's life published in 285BCE also drew on Alexander's own daily journal. Arrian's other main source was Aristobulos of Phocis, whose biography of Alexander appeared ca. 300BCE. Arrian writes, "wherever Ptolemy and Aristobulos in their histories of Alexander have given the same account I have followed it on the assumption of its accuracy." The anecdotal *Life of Alexander*, written by the historian and essayist Plutarch of Chaeronea (ca. 46–120CE), is based on the writings of a number of authors, including Callisthenes, Aristobulos, Chares, and Onesicritus, whose work is now known only from fragments.

Alexander's legend has proved remarkably durable. Modern Greek fishermen invoke his name to calm storms at sea, while, at the other end of his former empire, the warlords of Afghanistan are said still to fight beneath a flag they claim was once his. In whatever form his memory lingers, Alexander the Great, son of the gods, was undoubtedly one of the most remarkable men ever to have lived.

Alan Fildes and Joann Fletcher

Alexander the Great marched his army out of Macedonia and fought his way through Persian territory and into Egypt, where he was crowned as Pharaoh. Following his victory at the Battle of Gaugamela in 331BCE, the new Great King of Persia led his army across a further 11,000 miles of terrain, from scorching desert to waterlogged marshlands to freezing snow. Alexander created an empire that stretched across three continents and covered an area of some two million square miles (five million square kilometers), from Greece to the Punjab, and from the Danube to Nubia. The king never returned to Europe—he died in Babylon in 323BCE.

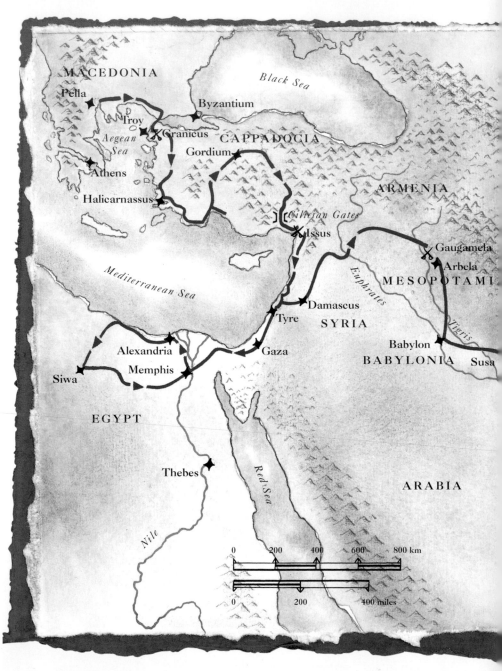

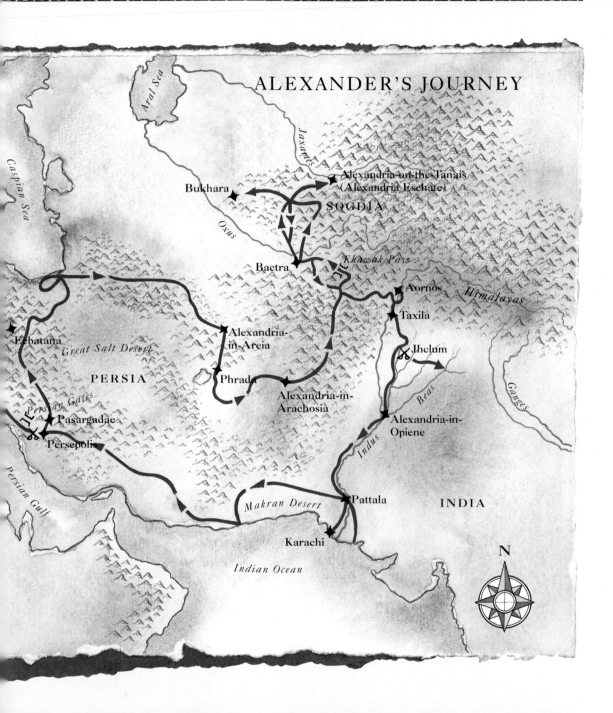

ALEXANDER'S JOURNEY

Aral Sea

Caspian Sea

Jaxartes

Bukhara

Alexandria-on-the-Tanais
(Alexandria Eschate)

SOGDIA

Oxus

Khawak Pass

Bactra

Aornos

Himalayas

Taxila

Ecbatana

Great Salt Desert

Alexandria-
in-Areia

Jhelum

PERSIA

Persian Gates

Phrada

Alexandria-in-
Arachosia

Beas

Pasargadae

Alexandria-in-
Opiene

Persepolis

Ganges

Persian Gulf

Indus

Makran Desert

Pattala

INDIA

Karachi

Indian Ocean

N

CHAPTER ONE

THE PRINCE
OF MACEDON

359–335 BCE

An ancient Macedonian marble statue depicting a young rider. This idealized
portrayal of athletic youth comes from the same culture that produced Alexander,
heir to the Macedonian throne and future conqueror of the known world.

KINGS OF THE MOUNTAIN REALM

Located in the northern extremity of Greece, and cut off from its neighbors by its mountainous terrain, ancient Macedonia's relative isolation produced a distinctly separate culture. Although the Macedonians spoke a Greek dialect, worshiped Greek gods, and traced their nation's origins from Macedon, son of Zeus, their customs and northern Doric accent were markedly different from those of the people of the rest of Greece, who saw Macedonia as a largely insignificant, backward monarchy, to be looked upon with suspicion. Yet this was the kingdom that produced Alexander the Great, the most powerful ruler Greece would ever know.

Among the ivory statuettes of the Macedonian royal family from Philip II's tomb at Vergina was this head of the king himself, suggesting the scarring which resulted from the loss of his right eye during the siege of Methone in 354BCE. By transforming a feuding, tribal kingdom into an invincible superpower, Philip was to pave the way for his son's even more remarkable achievements.

When not participating in military activities, members of the Macedonian warrior élite indulged to excess their other passions of hunting, womanizing, feasting, and drinking. Yet Macedonian rulers were also keen to promote Greek values—their court attracted artists, engineers, musicians, playwrights, and philosophers from all over the ancient world.

Originally based at the ancient dynastic capital Aegae (modern Vergina), the court was presided over by the king, who was the representative of the people and the commander-in-chief of the military forces. New rulers were chosen by an assembly made up of members of the warrior élite. The élite consisted of male members of aristocratic households, the "Companions" (*Hetairoi*), and the inner circle of royal "Friends" (*Philoi*) selected by the king. The heir or regent was usually the king's eldest son, yet this was not always the case, and the royal succession often entailed intrigue, deception, and even murder.

The earliest Macedonian royal lineage can be traced to the seventh-century BCE king Perdiccas, who was followed by Argaios (the founder of

the Argead dynasty). The first Alexander of Macedon (who reigned ca. 498–454BCE) was given "rule over the whole region between Mount Olympus and Mount Haemus [in northern Thrace]" by the Persian king Xerxes (486–465BCE), although the Macedonian monarch was to greatly expand his northern territories after the Persian defeat at the Battle of Plataea in 479BCE. Over the next century, nine kings ruled over a volatile Macedonia. Archelaus I (414–399BCE) moved the capital to Pella on the banks of the Loudias river. The grandson of Alexander I, Amyntas II (394–370BCE) strengthened Macedonia's defences against the ever-present threat posed by the half-subjugated Illyrians to the west.

At his death, Amyntas III left three sons, the eldest of whom, Alexander II ruled for less than a year before he was murdered by his mother's lover, Ptolemy Alorites. Perdiccas III avenged his brother by killing Ptolemy, only to die in battle in 359BCE. Amyntas III's third son—the 24-year-old Philip II (359–336BCE), future father of Alexander the Great—now came to power.

Macedonia, Greece, and the Aegean at the time of Philip II. Macedonia's highest peak is Mount Olympus, home of the ancient Olympian gods. In spring, against this ethereal backdrop of snow-capped peaks, melting waters transform into torrents, which rage down pine-clad ravines and pour into the Axius and Haliacmon rivers. Dissecting the rich Emathian floodplain, these mighty rivers flow out into the Aegean's deep Thermaic Gulf.

359–345BCE

WEDDINGS, PLOTS, AND PRINCES

On the death of his brother Perdiccas III in 359BCE, Philip was elected to act as regent for Perdiccas' infant son Amyntas. The Macedonian élite urgently needed an able leader to defend the kingdom against the Illyrian tribes, who were preparing to invade Macedonia yet again. Lacking direct leadership, the Macedonian army was still suffering from its humbling defeat at the hands of the Illyrians in the spring. Between 359 and 358BCE Philip spent most of his time, from his military headquarters in the royal capital of Pella, transforming his newly acquired troops into an efficient fighting force.

In order to secure his position in Macedonia, Philip disposed of the most dangerous of his half-brothers through execution or banishment. He was then able to set out to secure his country's vulnerable borders. In the spring of 358BCE the rejuvenated Macedonian army, led by Philip, invaded Paeonia to the northeast of the Axius river and defeated his old adversary Lyppeios. By campaigning into the summer, Philip was also able to finally defeat Bardylis, king of the Illyrians. The first invasion of Thessaly brought 358BCE to a jubilant close. In early 357BCE the Macedonians captured the Athenian-controlled Amphipolis.

In the fall of 357BCE Philip married the daughter of King Neoptolemus of Epirus (see page 16), giving his bride the Macedonian name "Olympias." Her main duty was to produce a male heir; Philip's first two wives had both died childless. Olympias soon conceived—legend has it that she felt herself impregnated by a thunderbolt as fire flooded her body before spreading out across the earth, while Philip was said to have dreamed he had sealed her womb with the image of a lion. When their first child, Alexander, was born on 20 or 26 July 356BCE, his father was away campaigning, and had just taken the city of Potidaea in the peninsula of Chalcidice. Victorious, Philip returned home to Pella and was immediately hailed King of Macedon by the army—his teenage nephew Amyntas had no choice but to formally relinquish his claim to the throne.

Alexander was raised in the beautiful marble palace at Pella, with its elegant murals, mosaics, and gardens. For the first seven years of his life, the prince was cared for by his nurse Lanice, sister of Cleitus (see page 91), the commander of the royal squadron of the Companion Cavalry. When the time came for the boy's education to begin, Olympias entrusted him to her kinsman Leonidas (see page 20). Alexander benefited enormously from the cosmopolitan nature of life at court, where he met visitors from all corners of the Greek world, Asia Minor, Egypt, and Persia.

Philip and Olympias had one more child together—a daughter called Cleopatra—before their turbulent relationship developed into open hostility. Philip's subsequent marriages and frequent affairs with both men and women only increased Olympias' enmity towards him. In contrast, the queen loved her son deeply. She even told Alexander that his true father was Zeus, king of the gods. Although it is hard to know what effect such a revelation may have had on the young boy's mind, the idea of his divine origins seems to have inspired him to superhuman deeds throughout his life.

The young Alexander was not the only prince at court—there were a number of other possible heirs to the throne, including Amyntas, who Philip married off to one of his own daughters by an Illyrian mistress. In typical royal Macedonian fashion, Philip had seven wives with whom he had several sons. Among Alexander's half-brothers was the son of the "humbly-born" Philinna of Larissa, Philip Arrhidaeus (see page 155), who was generally described as "weak-minded."

This marble head of King Philip II of Macedon is a copy of a 4th-century BCE Greek original. Philip was a robust, bearded warrior, unlike his son, Alexander the Great, who was rather more androgynous with his long hair, smooth complexion and large, wide eyes (see pages 106–9).

OLYMPIAS, DAUGHTER OF ACHILLES

In a rare respite from his endless campaigning, the 27-year-old Philip of Macedon visited Samothrace in 358BCE. This remote island was the venue for the annual religious festival known as the Mysteries, which drew pilgrims from all over the ancient world to worship the elemental powers. Among the pilgrims was Princess Polyxena Myrtale (later renamed Olympias) of Epirus, whose father's death had left her under the protection of her uncle King Arybbas. A devotee of mystic rituals, the princess was an eager participant in the torch-lit fertility rites, and it was at the island's dramatic mountain-top shrine that Philip fell in love with her.

Like Macedonia, Epirus was a feudal kingdom controlled by tribal loyalties, and each tribe traced its descent from one of the twelve Olympian gods. The Molossian royal family of Olympias also claimed the greatest of Greek heroes, Achilles (see page 22), as an ancestor, while her father was said to be of the same line as Helen of Troy.

Queen Olympias appears in raised relief on this gold medallion from the 3rd-century BCE Aboukir treasure (unfortunately, there are no contemporary likenesses of the queen).

The religious life of the Macedonian court was already steeped in mysticism when the young Olympias arrived there. A century earlier, the Athenian playwright Euripides had been inspired to write his greatest work, the powerful and disturbing *The Bacchae*, while living in Macedonia. Olympias must have found her spiritual home in Pella, for she was an incredibly devout woman who honored the gods on a daily basis, a practice her son would emulate. (Mother and son showed particular respect for Zeus, whose oracle was located in Olympias' home city of Dodona.) The queen had an emotional, volatile, and even violent temperament, and was an enthusiastic follower of Dionysus, best known as the god of wine and revelry. Dionysus was worshiped by his female devotees as the personification of the life-force itself and, at its most extreme, this worship frequently bordered on madness. Olympias often led such rites, accompanied by tame snakes, which, wrote Plutarch, " ... would lie concealed then rear their heads and coil themselves around the wands and garlands of the women in order to terrify the men."

Although Olympias' propensity for states of ritual possession was no doubt exaggerated to some extent by her detractors, she seems to have deserved her reputation for ruthlessness. She was certainly capable of resorting to violence in order to dispose of rivals, some of whom she is said to have poisoned or even roasted alive (see page 33). However, such actions were not uncommon features of ancient Macedonian power struggles. Philip's own mother, Eurydice, had been implicated in the deaths of her husband Amyntas III and her sons Alexander II and Perdiccas III.

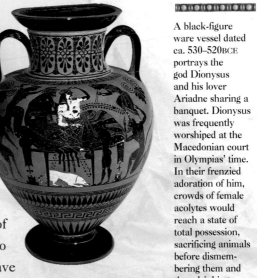

A black-figure ware vessel dated ca. 530–520BCE portrays the god Dionysus and his lover Ariadne sharing a banquet. Dionysus was frequently worshiped at the Macedonian court in Olympias' time. In their frenzied adoration of him, crowds of female acolytes would reach a state of total possession, sacrificing animals before dismembering them and then drinking their blood.

MOTHER AND SON

Olympias was determined to secure the throne for her only son, her love for whom was all-consuming. Alexander sometimes mirrored his mother's tendency for dramatic and emotional behavior.

Alexander was always close to Olympias, and many of his inner circle were associated with her family. Mother and son continued a written correspondence throughout his campaigns—the mixture of warmth and rebukes contained in their letters no doubt reflects their earlier life together in Macedonia. Irritated by his mother's running disputes with his deputy Antipater, Alexander once grumbled that she asked too great a price of his patience in return for the nine months she had carried him. Yet when Antipater wrote to Alexander to complain of Olympias' interference in matters of state, Alexander exclaimed that "one tear shed by my mother would wipe out ten thousand letters such as this." Plutarch records how, in one of her more interfering missives to her son, Olympias wrote, "I wish you would find other ways of rewarding those you love and honor. You make them all the equal of kings and enable them to make plenty of friends while leaving yourself without any!"

Alexander sent his mother and sister Cleopatra many of the spoils of his battles, described by Plutarch as, "drinking vessels, purple hangings, and other such plunder." In his absence, they in turn regularly sent offerings and dedications to the gods on Alexander's behalf to keep him safe.

"MACEDONIA IS TOO SMALL!"

By 348BCE, Philip II had taken control of Thessaly and Thrace, where he executed his surviving half-brothers for their part in an Athenian-backed rebellion. Two years later, in the spring of 346BCE, Alexander appears in historical accounts for the first time as a boy of nine. The court at Pella was playing host to ambassadors from all over Greece, who had come to discuss peace between themselves and also the formation of an alliance against their common enemy, Persia. After the envoys had dined with Philip, Alexander was brought in to entertain them. The prince showed great maturity and, according to a report by Aeschines, "he played the lyre and recited, then debated with another boy."

Horses were highly prized by the Greeks and were often portrayed in works of art such as this marble horse head, which dates from the late 5th century BCE. Alexander's taming of Bucephalas (see right), the horse that was to accompany him for the next twenty years, is often described as marking the end of the young prince's boyhood.

The evening with the Greek envoys is not the only occasion on which the future king is reported to have impressed visitors. The taming of the horse Bucephalas also proved the prince's prowess in a spectacular and very public way. In ca. 345BCE, a friend of Philip's bought him an expensive black thoroughbred stallion. Although Bucephalas was already 12 years old, no-one had ever been able to break him in. His erratic behavior as the royal grooms brought him out onto the plain made Philip lose his patience, and he ordered that the horse be led away.

According to Plutarch, the young Alexander remarked loudly, "What a horse they are losing, just because they don't know the best way to handle him, or if they do they dare not try." "Do you think you can manage horses better than they can?" Philip asked his son. "Well I could certainly manage this one better than they can!" Alexander replied. "But if you cannot what will be the consequence of your impertinence?" retorted his father. "I will pay what the horse cost," said Alexander, much to the amusement of the assembled group. Plutarch describes how, "Alexander went right up to Bucephalas and took hold of his bridle, turning him toward the sun, for he had noticed that the horse had been shying away from its own shadow ... Throwing aside his cloak he vaulted up on to his back ... At first Philip and his Companions watched with bated breath ... until they saw Alexander end the gallop, turn, and ride back toward them jubilant and triumphant. The group burst into loud applause, while Philip, we are told, wept with joy and pride. When his son dismounted he kissed him and uttered the prophetic words, 'My boy, you must find a kingdom big enough for your ambitions. Macedonia is just too small for you.'"

THE PRINCE AND THE LION

Lion hunting was a popular pastime among the Macedonian élite. Following in a long tradition of ancient kings from countries as diverse as Egypt and Persia, Prince Alexander in particular regarded the lion as a worthy opponent.

On one hunting trip with his Companions, Alexander was also accompanied by an envoy from Sparta, the most warlike of all Greek states. Ever keen to show off his physical skills, the prince speared a great lion, at which the Spartan envoy remarked, "Alexander, you fought bravely with this lion to decide which of you should be king." Plutarch describes how Alexander's friend Craterus even commemorated the moment by commissioning the official royal sculptor Lysippus to create a bronze sculpture of Alexander fighting the lion with his pet hound.

Lysippus' statue of Alexander's lion hunt inspired this mosaic scene, dated ca. 320BCE, from Pella. The figure on the left is identified as Alexander; Craterus is on the right.

THE PHILOSOPHER'S STUDENT

At the age of seven, Alexander left the care of his nurse Lanice to undergo a rigorous education at the hands of his mother's kinsman Leonidas. The latter proved a hard task-master—Plutarch notes that Alexander later remembered how the tutor, "used to come and look through my bedding boxes and clothes chests to see that my mother did not hide any luxuries for me." Indeed, Leonidas' royal pupil appears to have harbored a degree of resentment toward his first teacher long after the end of his schooling. Fifteen years after Leonidas made a sarcastic comment about the boy's lavish use of incense during rituals, Alexander (who never forgot a slight) sent his old master 16 tons of incense with the message, "I have sent you plenty of myrrh and frankincense, so you need never be mean toward the gods again."

His schooldays saw the beginning of Alexander's love of the arts—as an adult he would become a great patron of musicians, actors, painters, and literary figures. During his early military training, the young prince was watched over by the Acarnanian courtier Lysimachus, who styled himself as Phoenix to Alexander's Achilles, reflecting the youngster's life-long passion for Homer's *Iliad* (see page 22). Alexander also enjoyed reading the dramatic tragedies of Aeschylus and Sophocles, and knew the plays of Euripides by heart. Aelian recorded that the young prince, who was skilled in playing the lyre, had a clear singing voice as a boy. However, King Philip once remarked that his son should be ashamed of having such a sweet voice, after which Alexander was never known to sing again.

Following Alexander's initial tuition under the guidance of Leonidas, Philip decided it was time for his 13-year-old son to graduate to higher education. Because of the unstable political situation, it was considered dangerous to send Alexander to the renowned Academy in Athens, so the king sent for an Athenian tutor to come to Macedonia. This decision was

The Greek philosopher Aristotle acted as tutor to the precocious young Alexander, giving him lessons in subjects as diverse as geography, zoology, politics, and medicine. This Roman alabaster bust of Aristotle is copied from a 4th-century BCE Greek bronze.

to result in one of the most significant encounters in history for, although the head of the Athens Academy offered to resign in order to take up the prestigious post of royal tutor, Philip instead chose the still largely unknown philosopher Aristotle. The world's greatest intellectual and greatest conqueror were thus brought together in an atmosphere of mutual admiration and respect. Aristotle was later quoted as saying, "A wise man should fall in love, take part in politics, and live with a king," suggesting that he had fond memories of his time at the royal court. Alexander certainly seems to have held his tutor in high esteem—until his death the king slept with a copy of Homer's *Iliad*, annotated by Aristotle, beneath his pillow.

When he arrived in Macedonia, Aristotle was in his early forties, and was described as "thin-legged and small-eyed." As a student of Plato— who had died just four years earlier—Aristotle was the heir to the former's intellectual prominence. As well as his impressive academic credentials, Aristotle also had the advantage of being greatly trusted by Philip, as his father had served as the doctor to the Macedonian royal house.

Philip gave his son's tutor a fine house in Mieza near modern Naoussa.

THE PRINCELY ARTS

Alexander was also taught the physical skills necessary to become a warrior king. As a boy, he displayed a great aptitude for sports and combat. Rigorous training under his mother's kinsman Leonidas ensured the young prince was highly proficient in the use of the *sarissa*, the mighty Macedonian lance, together with the javelin, bow, and quarter-staff. Also a fine runner, Alexander was invited to compete at Olympia but would only take part, "if I have kings to run against me." In addition to his athletic prowess, the prince revealed great horsemanship when he broke in his own horse, Bucephalas (see pages 18–19).

This 5th-century BCE bowl depicts a young Greek athlete taking oil from an amphora to rub onto his skin before a race.

DREAMING OF THE *ILIAD*

From childhood, Alexander loved Homer's epic sagas the *Iliad* and the *Odyssey*, and was inspired by their tales of the mighty deeds of gods and heroes during the Trojan War and its aftermath. As the prince grew up, he began to model himself on the *Iliad*'s Achilles, the greatest of all Greek heroes. When, as a young king embarking on the invasion of Asia, Alexander visited Troy, he made a special pilgrimage to Achilles' tomb (see page 42).

Alexander claimed Achilles as an ancestor on his mother's side (see page 16) and never missed an opportunity to compare himself to his hero. The parallels between the two are certainly striking: both were believed to be the sons of mortal women and gods; both had lifelong male partners who died before them; both successfully led the Greeks against the barbarian enemy; and both died young in their attempts to surpass those around them. Indeed, one of Alexander's favorite lines from Homer is said to have been, "Ever to be best and stand far above all others."

Alexander's own copy of the *Iliad*, annotated by Aristotle (see page 21), was one of his most prized possessions. As well as reading it for pleasure, he regarded it as "a handbook on the art of war," and kept it in a precious jewel-encrusted gold casket that had once belonged to the Persian king Darius.

A detail of a painted, Attic black-figure vase scene (ca. 530BCE) depicting Achilles about to spear an enemy he recognizes only too late as female—the Amazon warrior Penthisilia.

Here, in the peaceful Temple of the Nymphs and "Gardens of Midas" deep in the Macedonian countryside, Prince Alexander received a three-year education which fully equiped him for empire-building.

Aristotle may have occasionally been frustrated by his exuberant charge. Remarks made by the philosopher after his time at Mieza, include: "A young man is not the right sort of person to listen to political science; he has no experience of life"; "because he [the young man] still follows his emotions, he will listen to no purpose"; and "the young think they know it all already." In spite of this, it seems clear that Aristotle's political teachings provided Alexander with a solid background in law and statecraft. The philosopher's image of the highly principled "great-souled man" also gave the future king the model he sought to emulate for the rest of his life.

Aristotle's metaphysical revelations also provided inspiration and guidance for Alexander, so much so that when the conqueror later learned that the philosopher had published on the subject, he wrote him a letter bluntly asking, "What advantage would I have over other men if these theories in which I have been trained are made common property? I would rather excel the rest of mankind in my knowledge of what is best than in the extent of my power."

Alexander's passion for scientific exploration and discovery was fuelled by his tutor. Aristotle's scientific expertise stemmed partly from his family's medical background, and he imbued Alexander with an understanding of medicine that the latter would later put to good use among his troops. Pupil and teacher also shared a passion for natural history, botany, and zoology. During his campaigns, the conqueror Alexander would often collect specimens of flora and fauna to send to his old tutor.

Aristotle held the conventional Greek view of male superiority and was a proponent of the accepted wisdom that men's most important relationships, platonic or otherwise, should be with other men. Alexander's own lifetime companion Hephaestion (see page 96) was almost certainly a fellow student at Mieza and, like Alexander, he corresponded with his old tutor after Aristotle's return to Athens. Chief among the boys' companions was the elder Ptolemy, close friend and rumored half-brother of Alexander (Ptolemy's mother Arsinoe and Philip II had enjoyed a brief liaison as teenagers), who was no doubt inspired in his future roles as pharaoh of Egypt and historian by Aristotle's early influence.

———— 340BCE ————

TRIUMPHS OF THE YOUNG REGENT

An ancient bronze (opposite) portrays Alexander astride Bucephalas at the head of a battle charge (see also page 42). Plutarch wrote of the prince, " ... his passionate desire for fame implanted in him a pride and a grandeur of vision which went far beyond his years ... his choice was a life of struggle, of wars, and of unrelenting ambition."

During the three and a half years that Alexander spent studying at Mieza with Aristotle (see pages 20–23), King Philip was working to increase Macedonia's strength at home and abroad. This inevitably led to a marked deterioration in relations with the rest of Greece. The Athenians were driven to propose the formation of a new Anti-Macedonian League, which was to include Macedonia's supposed allies, the Greek state of Thebes in Boeotia and Byzantium in Asia Minor. Such was their fear of Macedonia, members of the League even accepted funds from their traditional enemy, Persia.

Although Philip faced overwhelming odds, he was not easily intimidated. He proposed that Byzantium and Macedonia form an alliance against the Athenians, whose superior naval force was already attacking Macedonian interests in the Dardanelles. Byzantium's inevitable refusal gave Philip the excuse he needed—he began to ready the fleet he had been preparing.

As king, Philip was expected to lead his forces in person, and therefore needed to leave Macedonia in the hands of someone he trusted. This was the perfect opportunity for him to test the abilities of his 16-year-old son. Alexander was recalled from Mieza, and in 340BCE he was officially appointed as Regent of Macedon—a challenge the prince had been longing for. He was now officially recognized as Crown Prince, Philip's chosen successor. As "Keeper of the Royal Seal," Alexander was left in complete control of Macedonia, with Philip's trusted official Antipater as adviser.

No sooner had the king left for Byzantium than the border tribes in northeastern Macedonia seized the opportunity to rebel yet again, threatening Macedonia's supply routes in the region. Alexander set off immediately to defend the kingdom, keen to make an example of the rebels. Two years earlier, Alexander had had his first military experience when he had acted as a page (attending the king and fighting near him in battle). He was soon to prove that he was more than capable of leading an army.

In an impressive display of military prowess, Alexander soundly defeated the Thracian Maedi. He took their city, drove out its inhabitants, and replaced them with Greek settlers, creating a Macedonian outpost which he renamed Alexandropolis. The first of many such self-named cities (see pages 60–61), this was a clear indication of the teenager's aspirations.

In recognition of his success, Philip promoted Alexander to the rank of general. Father and son fought side by side during the arduous Thracian campaigns of 340–339BCE, extending Macedonia's power to the Dardanelles. Alexander

later recalled how he saved Philip's life during one of these battles. After being wounded, Philip fell and was forced to feign death. The young general protected the king with his shield, slaying his attackers. Alexander later complained that this was a fact "his father had never been man enough to admit, being unwilling to owe his life to his son."

HIS FATHER'S SON

Alexander's relationship with his father was extremely ambiguous. As Philip repeatedly slighted Olympias by taking wife after wife, Alexander seems to have taken comfort from the idea that he was different and special, a child of the gods (see page 15). Later in life he even referred to Philip as "my so-called father."

Yet, however different in looks and temperament, father and son shared the same yearning for greatness. Alexander genuinely admired Philip, whose achievements he sought to emulate and even surpass. As a young boy, he is said to have complained, "My father will forestall me in everything until there will be nothing great left to do in the entire world!" Philip was immensely proud of his precocious son, and, according to Plutarch, "became extravagantly fond of him, so much so that he took pleasure in hearing the Macedonians speak of Alexander as their king and Philip as their general."

— 339–338BCE —

THE FALL OF ATHENS

In the summer of 339BCE Philip caught the allied forces of the Anti-Macedonian League by surprise when he swept into central Greece at the head of his army and occupied Elatea on the route between Athens and Thebes. The two cities formed a coalition: supported by a 10,000-strong mercenary force, they planned to oppose the Macedonian army on land, despite the fact that Athens' real power lay with her fleet. However, in a night attack, Philip overcame the mercenary forces and took the town of Amphissa near Delphi.

The Athenians and Thebans fell back to the site of Chaeronea and drew up their line of defence between the citadel and the Cephisus river. Their 2,000-strong cavalry force was equal to that of the Macedonians, and they outnumbered Philip's 30,000-strong infantry by 5,000 men. At dawn on 4 August 338BCE the two sides met in what has often been described as one of the most decisive encounters in Greek history.

When the Macedonian infantry appeared to back away, the Athenians were fooled and launched themselves toward the enemy. Alexander's charge at the head of the Companion Cavalry promptly cut the Athenians off from their Theban allies. At the same time, Philip's forces began to advance and attack in a classic Macedonian phalanx maneuver. Alexander's second charge scattered the Boeotian cavalry, then decimated the élite Theban Sacred Band while the rest of the Greeks fled the field.

Although the Thebans were to pay a high price for defeat (see caption, opposite), Philip was magnanimous toward the humiliated Athenians. His generous peace terms reflected his desire for a reconciliation, which was vital if a Macedonian-led united Greek campaign against Persia were to succeed. In return for becoming Macedonia's ally, Athens' 2,000 prisoners

of war were released without ransom, and the ashes of more than 1,000 of their fallen countrymen were returned home by Alexander himself.

In early September, Philip marched to Corinth, where he organized a peace conference to formalize plans for a Macedonian-led crusade against Persia. Representatives from all the southern states except Sparta attended. Philip forced them to make peace and form a Hellenic League, which was required to form an alliance with Macedonia and vote its king—and his descendants—"Supreme Commander of Greek Forces." In reality, this gave the Macedonian ruler unlimited powers over the city-states.

AN ARMY FOR THE EAST

Well before his accession, Philip II had realized the need for a reliable fighting force on which his country could depend. As king, he transformed his army into a tough, highly disciplined body of soldiers, which enabled him to turn Macedonia itself into a major military power.

As a teenager, when he was a diplomatic hostage in Thebes, Philip had been inspired by the military genius of the great Theban general Epaminondas and the prowess of the élite Sacred Band (see page 27). However, when he was elected king in 359BCE, he inherited a force that was little more than a weak, undisciplined rabble. The new leader's methods for reforming his army are reported by Diodorus Siculus, "He improved their formations and equiped his troops with the appropriate weapons of war, holding frequent exercises under arms and competitions of physical fitness." Within months of his accession, Philip's new regime had produced a marked improvement in attitude and discipline.

As the king's ceaseless campaigning began to lay the foundations for a future empire, new wealth was used to fund military reforms, and prisoners

The basic Macedonian phalanx was made up of 16 battalions of 256 pikemen arranged in ranks 16 men wide and 16 deep. The phalanx was dependant upon the ability of its well-drilled troops to move precisely together, and could only advance at a steady march.

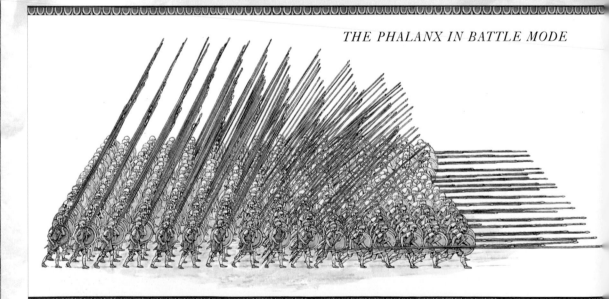

THE PHALANX IN BATTLE MODE

of war were set to work on the land to allow Macedonians to become full-time soldiers rather than farmers. Macedonia was rapidly acquiring a large, professional army at a time when, in the rest of Greece, the possession of a full-time standing army was seen as a sign of tyranny.

During his reign (359–336BCE), Philip increased the number of infantry soldiers in the standing army from 10,000 to 24,000. Leading infantry troops were given the title "Foot Companions," equal in standing to their counterparts in the cavalry. The best 3,000 infantry soldiers, known as "Royal Shield Bearers," formed the finest infantry force in the ancient world.

Macedonia's growing army was equiped with the latest weaponry, chief among which was the *sarissa*, an extremely long, cornel-wood pike tipped with an iron blade. Infantry soldiers, arranged in the massed ranks of the phalanx formation (see illustration, opposite), learned to wield the *sarissa* with deadly efficiency. The phalanx combination of spear and shield created a bristling, impenetrable wall which advanced into enemy lines to the war cry "Alalalalai." When deployed on level ground, the Macedonian phalanx proved unbeatable.

By the end of his reign, Philip had also increased the size of the cavalry from 600 to a 3,500-strong mounted force, 2,000 of whom were the famed Thessalian cavalry. Wearing helmets and light body armor, the heavy cavalry were armed with fearsome thrusting spears and short swords. The light cavalry, equiped with blade-tipped javelins, were often deployed on reconnaissance, a crucial part of ancient warfare. The king also employed a corps of engineers, headed by Polyeidus of Thessaly, to develop new methods of siege warfare, such as the 120-foot (36-meter) high siege tower. Philip revolutionized such techniques to successfully besiege Amphipolis, Pydna, and Potdaia in 357–356BCE.

All these developments would later be of immense significance to Alexander as he advanced into Asia. By creating such invincible forces, and devising a strategy based on careful planning combined with speedy attack, Philip gave his son the means of taking on the world.

A bronze Greek helmet and breast-plate (cuirass), dated 4th–3rd century BCE. Metal breastplates were standard armor for members of the Macedonian Companion cavalry, and were often provided for officers of the Companion infantry. However, it was only under Alexander that breastplates became standard issue for the entire army.

337–336BCE

EXILE IN EPIRUS

Philip returned to Macedonia at the end of 338BCE. Early the next year he declared war on Persia. It was also in 337BCE that the king fell in love with Cleopatra, the young niece of the Companion Attalus. Set on marriage, Philip gave his bride-to-be the honorific name Eurydice, after his own mother. The status of members of the Attalid family was greatly enhanced by this union. Plutarch recounts how, at the marriage banquet, Attalus (who had consumed a large amount of strong local wine) drank the newly-weds' health and loudly invited all Macedonians to pray to the gods that the couple would soon produce "a legitimate heir."

True to character, Alexander reacted with instant fury to this public slur on his honor and on that of his Epirot mother. He screamed, "So am I a bastard, then?" and hurled his cup at Attalus, who threw his back at Alexander. In the ensuing brawl Philip had to intervene to prevent bloodshed. As Alexander demanded satisfaction, Philip lost his temper with the prince. Alexander insulted his father, who was sufficiently provoked to draw his sword, and as an inebriated Philip lurched forward to retaliate, he tripped and fell. His son, standing over him, scoffed, "Look at him, the man preparing to cross from Europe to Asia and he can't even get from one table to another."

With this, Alexander turned and stormed out. Accompanied by his closest friends and his mother, he left the palace and crossed the south-west border into Epirus. Having delivered Olympias to her brother King Alexander at his court in Dodona, the prince rode north to Illyria. This had been a center of rebellion in Philip's earlier years, and Alexander's choice of destination was no doubt calculated to alarm his father. As long as Philip's embittered yet popular son remained the guest of a recently

hostile power, and his estranged wife was plotting revenge in Epirus, the king would be unable
to leave Macedonia unguarded. He would be
forced to place his Persian campaign on hold.

The stalemate between father and son was
eventually broken by a family friend who acted
as go-between. At Philip's summons, Alexander
and Olympias returned to Pella and were reinstated at court. However, with Attalus and his
clan growing increasingly powerful, Alexander's
inheritance was only secure until Eurydice produced a male child. Philip's new wife had been
with child at the time of their wedding, and had
already given birth to a girl named Europa; by the
fall of 337BCE she was pregnant again.

Philip decided to send an advance force into
Asia Minor in the spring of 336BCE, led by
General Parmenio. Instead of giving Alexander a command position,
Philip placed his trust in Attalus, Parmenio's son-in-law. With a remit to
secure the Dardanelles, prepare supplies for the forthcoming invasion,
and liberate the Greek cities of Asia Minor from Persian rule, the army
marched south down the coast of Ionia. The cities of Chios, Erythrae, and
Ephesus all opened their gates in welcome.

Epirus, the land
of Olympias' birth.
It was here that
she was taken
by Alexander
following his
confrontation
with his father.

Philip sent enquiries to the oracle at
Delphi to ask whether he would
conquer the Persian Great King.
The oracle sent the following
answer: "Wreathed is the bull.
All is done. The sacrificer
awaits." The Macedonian king
chose to interpret these ambiguous words as confirmation of
his imminent success. However,
this could not have been further
from the truth—the person about to
be sacrificed was Philip himself.

This 3rd-century
BCE cameo depicts
Alexander (right)
and Olympias.
Ever mindful of his
mother's feelings,
Alexander is said
to have told Philip
at his marriage
to Eurydice,
"When my mother
remarries I'll
invite *you* to
her wedding."

A short sword, similar to this Achaemenid-period Persian dagger, was used to kill Philip. Athenians known to be in league with Persia were believed to be conspirators in the assassination plot; Alexander always suspected the Persians of involvement.

336–335BCE

ASSASSINATION IN THE THEATER

At the height of the summer of 336BCE, the Macedonian royal family met at Aegae to celebrate the marriage of Philip and Olympias' daughter Cleopatra to Alexander, King of Epirus. Philip needed a royal alliance with Epirus to replace his failed marriage to Olympias. The relationship between the king of Macedonia and his formidable queen had irrevocably broken down, and the situation had become even more tense when, a few weeks earlier, Philip's new wife Eurydice had given birth to a boy. Philip is said to have named his son Caranus after the founder of the royal dynasty.

Philip of Macedon—now at the peak of his power—was in buoyant mood. His daughter's wedding celebrations were to culminate in the theater at Aegae in a procession led by statues of the 12 Olympian gods followed by a figure representing Philip. The king himself would then enter the arena, flanked by his son and his brother-in-law. Yet, at the very last moment, Philip changed his plans, sent the two Alexanders ahead of him, and prepared to make his grand entrance alone. It was at this moment that Pausanias, the captain of the bodyguard, struck Philip between the ribs with a short sword, killing him outright. In the ensuing confusion, three bodyguards pursued the assassin, who was fleeing toward the city gates where he had horses waiting. He was killed before he could reach them.

News of Philip's assassination spread rapidly. As rebellions began to erupt to the north and south, it became imperative to elect a new king. The decision of the royal household's high-ranking military men was an easy one. Philip had been preparing Alexander for this day all his life; the 20-year-old prince had repeatedly proved his worth and had earned the respect and confidence of the Macedonian élite.

The first duty of the new King Alexander III of Macedon was to lead the enquiry into his father's murder. The circumstances of Philip's death remain far from clear. Inevitably, some have laid the blame squarely at Olympias' door. She had the most to gain from the removal of the husband who had publicly humiliated her, and whose death would result in her beloved son's accession to the throne. It has even been suggested that Alexander had a hand in his father's assassination, but such a calculated act of patricide—the most serious crime in the eyes of the gods—would have been totally out of character for the prince.

Some sources claim that Pausanias' crime was simply one of passion, following his replacement in Philip's affections by a younger man. Yet the fact that there were a number of horses waiting for the assassin suggests that he had not acted alone. Alexander's own life was at risk until Pausanias' accomplices were caught. The new king took the opportunity to remove all those he suspected of plotting against both Philip and himself.

All alleged crimes were dealt with by Macedonia's constitutional law. The Assembly concluded that Pausanias had been in league with two sons of Aeropus (see page 13), and had conspired with the hated Attalus (see page 30) to assassinate Philip. Aeropus' sons were executed. Attalus was killed trying to resist arrest, and was posthumously condemned as a traitor. His male blood relatives—including the baby Caranus, born to Philip and Attalus' niece only days before—were all executed under the law of treason. Although the Attalid womenfolk were to be spared, Eurydice met her death at the hands of a gleeful Olympias (if sensationalist contemporary reports are to be believed, Olympias roasted her rival alive over a brazier). Alexander's older cousin Amyntas (see page 15) was also found guilty of treason and executed in the summer of 335BCE.

Philip's funeral procession was led by Alexander with great ceremony. Alexander inaugurated annual sacrifices in honor of his father, although Philip's true memorial was to be his son's conquest of Persia.

Philip of Macedon's unplundered tomb has recently been discovered in the royal necropolis at Aegae (modern Vergina). The king's remains were interred in this gold chest, decorated with the star emblem of the Macedonian royal family and rosettes inlaid with blue glass. Among the sumptuous grave goods were: Philip's crown of gold oak leaves; two iron swords and a *sarissa*; horse trappings; an arrow quiver of gilded silver; an iron helmet and cuirass; gold-plated bronze greaves (long metal armor plates that protect the shins) embossed with scenes of warfare; gold and silver wine vessels; and ivory statuettes of the royal family, including Alexander and Olympias.

CHAPTER TWO

CONQUEROR OF THE EAST

335–331 BCE

Detail of Alexander, in resplendent armor, leading the cavalry charge
at the Battle of Issus from the so-called "Issus Mosaic," a Roman
copy from Pompeii of an original Greek painting by Philoxenus.

335–334BCE

THE LORD OF ALL GREECE

Having avenged his father, the newly crowned Alexander III set about establishing his authority within Macedonia. He exempted Macedonians from all public duties save military service. The young king also recalled all his friends from exile and gave them key posts in the new administration. Yet, although he managed to secure his position at home, Alexander was faced with wide-scale rebellion throughout the rest of Greece when, in time-honored fashion, the neighboring kingdoms began to take advantage of the transition between monarchs. The Greek city-states had refused to acknowledge Alexander's supremacy and were already planning a revolt against Macedonian authority, which they mistakenly assumed had ended with Philip's death.

However, it soon became clear that the new king of Macedonia was in no mood to relinquish any of his father's territories. With characteristic speed, Alexander marched into Thessaly. Victory was achieved without a fight and the Thessalians elected Alexander "Archon of Thessaly" for life.

Against the cautionary advice of his deputy Antipater, Alexander then marched south, much to the alarm of the Greek city-states, where Philip's death had been the cause of great celebration. Thrown into panic at Alexander's approach, they sent envoys to plead for pardon. Although Sparta and Argos began to rebel along with Thebes, their resistance quickly crumbled when the Macedonian army appeared at their gates.

In less than two months and without bloodshed, Alexander imposed his control over the key city-states. In order to formalize his position, he summoned a meeting of the Hellenic League at Corinth, during which the member states recognized him as Philip's successor and duly elected him "Supreme Commander of Greek Forces" at the head of the campaign against Persia. Only the Spartans (who were secretly plotting with the Persian king) refused to recognize Alexander's leadership, claiming that any such force should be led by them. With southern Greece under his control, Alexander spent the winter in Macedonia training the army. In spring 335BCE, leaving Macedonia in the capable hands of Antipater, the king set out with his army and a contingent of Thracian auxiliaries, determined to finally crush the rebellious border tribes still threatening his homeland.

Alexander led his army northeast to his father's military garrison at Philippopolis; at the Balkan range of Mount Haemus he encountered the tattooed Thracian forces. The Macedonian leader knew from his reconnaissance troops that the Thracians had secured the high ground, and had lined up wagons at the summit which, if unleashed, would cause chaos. Alexander ordered the heavy infantry to open their ranks to allow the wagons through. Soldiers in the narrower parts of the terrain were told to lie down and interlock their shields over them in "tortoise" formation. As predicted, the wagons were unleashed, but without the element of surprise

Alexander visited Delphi (below) to consult the famous oracle about his Persian campaign. He arrived on a day on which the oracle could not be approached, but he refused to wait. The priestess was forced to give in to his demands and, in exasperation, declared, "You are invincible, my son," which the young king took as a guarantee of his future success.

This detail of the relief on a Greek sarcophagus dated 360–350BCE depicts mourning women. A generation later, Alexander inflicted huge casualties on those who dared to rebel against Macedonia, and such scenes of grief and despair must have become commonplace across Greece.

they failed to achieve their desired effect. The Macedonians went on to kill 1,500 of the enemy.

Alexander now advanced into Triballian territory, where 3,000 enemy soldiers were cut down with the loss of only 51 Macedonians.

Three days later, Alexander reached the northern border of his empire on the banks of the Ister. On the other side of the river, the Celtic Getae had marshaled 4,000 cavalry and more than 10,000 foot soldiers. Alexander ordered his men to fill their tents with hay to make them buoyant and use them to cross the water by cover of darkness. At dawn, the enemy was quickly defeated. Alexander accepted the unconditional surren-der of the Getae and all the tribes in the area as far away as the Adriatic. Meanwhile, there came news of a serious uprising on the western border, where Cleitus of Illyria, the son of Philip's old enemy Bardylis, had formed an alliance with Glaucias of the Taulantians. After a rapid march westward, Alexander's troops reached Cleitus' hilltop fortress at Pelium, where, in spite of being trapped between the two enemy forces, the Macedonians were again victorious. The terrible massacre that followed put an end to Illyrian ambition once and for all.

During the months that Alexander spent campaigning on Macedonia's borders, the Greek city-states were busy plotting against him. Funded by Persia's new king, Darius III (see page 41), Demosthenes planned to sab-otage the anti-Persian campaign by keeping Alexander busy in Greece. The orator announced to the Athenian Assembly that Alexander and his entire army had been killed fighting the Triballians, hoping to spark off a general uprising. This false news quickly spread through Greece, and it was not long before rebellion began. The Thebans voted to join forces

ALEXANDER'S MEN

Alexander's key military advisers included old stalwarts who had served under his father. Among those who had fought alongside Philip was General Parmenio. Alexander, who needed Parmenio's support to gain the endorsement of Macedonia's nobility, gave the general's sons and brothers key posts in the new administration.

Antipater—another trusted official of the old school—was appointed to rule Macedonia in Alexander's absence. Other elder statesmen who were retained in the new regime included Antigonus Monophthalmus, "the One-Eyed,"

the governor of Phrygia, and the cavalry commander Cleitus "the Black" (see page 91).

However, Alexander's most trusted advisers were his own friends, especially Hephaestion (see page 96) and Craterus, who became the king's second-in-command after the death of Parmenio. Alexander also promoted Harpalus, who was made Royal Treasurer; Nearchus, who became governor of Lycia and later batallion commander of the guards and admiral of the fleet; and the philosopher Callisthenes, whom Alexander appointed as his official chronicler.

with Athens and Persia in order to overthrow Macedonian rule.

Alexander now had no choice but to march his tired army 250 miles (400 kilometers) south from Pelium to Thebes in an astonishing 13 days. When his offer of amnesty in exchange for the leaders of the revolt was refused, Alexander blocked the road out to Athens, and used his great siege engines to breach Thebes' city walls. Without reinforcements from the Athenians, the Theban defenders were overcome. Some managed to flee, but the remaining 6,000 were mercilessly butchered by Alexander's Phocian and Plataean auxiliaries. The king himself intervened to save the Theban priests, some of his father's old friends, and the descendants of the poet Pindar. However, most of their fellow citizens were not so lucky—a total of 20,000 Thebans were sold into slavery. Their city was razed to the ground.

The Macedonian ruler had clearly demonstrated that he would not tolerate any transgression against his authority. The Athenians were again thrown into panic, and assumed their own city would be next. To their amazement, they were spared—Alexander, who saw himself as the champion of Greece, did not want to be seen as a despot in the city that was the home of democracy and the most important Greek city-state.

Having secured the whole of Greece, the king was able to return home to begin the final preparations for his great crusade against Persia.

THE GREAT KINGS OF PERSIA

Contrary to Greek propaganda, the Persians were a highly sophisticated people. Their 200-year-old empire, which stretched from Greece to Afghanistan, and from Scythia down to Nubia, was a source of enormous wealth—the Persian monarch was the richest man on earth. At the heart of the empire lay the dazzling royal city of Persepolis (see pages 72–7). From the splendor of his palace, the mighty Great King of Persia ruled over a population of millions.

The huge Achaemenid Persian empire was created by Cyrus the Great (who ruled 548–529BCE). As the empire began to take over the Greek colonies in Asia Minor in 510BCE, Darius I (521–486BCE) invaded Greece itself. Having lost the Battle of Marathon in 490BCE, the Persians returned under Xerxes I (485–465BCE) to sack Athens in 480BCE, but were defeated

PERSIAN GOVERNMENT

A detail from a sarcophagus dated 410BCE depicting the characteristic dress of a Persian in power.

Persian expansion involved the absorption of individual countries whose internal structures remained largely intact. Only the top level of government was changed—the native king, pharaoh, or chief was replaced by the Great King's appointed governor (satrap). This retention of individual power structures across the empire maximized Persia's administrative efficiency by retaining established institutions and the native bureaucrats who ran them. The only difference was that the old institutions were co-ordinated by a Persian governor in the name of the Great King, on whose behalf taxes and tribute were collected.

Alexander was full of admiration for the Persians' ability to rule over such diverse peoples from a central point. Once he had claimed the title of "Great King" himself (see page 84), he had no qualms about adopting "Persian ways" when they promised to produce more efficient results than Greek-style methods, and the satrapal system remained largely intact.

A detail of a door relief from Persepolis portrays the majesty of a Persian monarch. Darius III was reputed to be 6.5 feet (2 meters) tall, which made him a giant by the standards of the ancient world. Plutarch describes the last Persian Great King as "a handsome man who towered above his companions."

later that year in the sea battle of Salamis, fixing the Persian empire's western border at the shore of the Dardanelles (Hellespont). In subsequent clashes with Greece the Persians met with sporadic resistance. Philip II of Macedon came to the throne at the same time as Artaxerxes III (Ochus) of Persia (358–338BCE), who funded the anti-Macedonian League (see page 24). Artaxerxes III was poisoned by his vizier Bagoas, who replaced the Great King with his young son Arses amid increasing anarchy. In spring 336BCE, Bagoas struck again, assassinating Arses.

With the direct royal line extinguished, the nobleman Codomannus was selected and crowned as Darius III. Arrian calls Darius, who was around 50 years old when he came to the throne, "the feeblest and most incompetant of men when it came to military matters"; his attempts to repel Alexander's invasion were certainly thwarted by overconfidence, fear, and irresolution. However, Darius seems to have been capable of political, if not military, wisdom: his first act on becoming king was to execute the traitorous Bagoas.

THE INVASION OF ASIA

By early 334BCE Alexander was ready to move against the Persian empire, and set out east at the head of a combined allied Greek force of 40,000 infantry and 6,000 cavalry. After 20 days they sailed across the Dardanelles; Alexander would never return to Europe. Once on Asian soil, the king led a small entourage to Troy, where he offered sacrifices to Athena, the city's patron goddess. With Hephaestion, Alexander then visited the tomb of his supposed ancestor, Achilles (see page 22). This was a calculated move—Alexander was drawing a comparison between Greece's heroic past and what he saw as a new age of glory, with himself cast as Achilles.

This late-Hellenistic bronze statuette from Herculaneum shows Alexander astride Bucephalas and is copied from Lysippus' statue set up at Dium to commemorate Alexander's victory at the Battle of the Granicus. The rudder indicates that Alexander had to cross the river before achieving victory.

In May Alexander's party joined up with the main body of the allied forces at Arisbe. The king gave orders to march east toward the Granicus river, beyond which the Persian army, under the command of Darius' nobles, was known to be waiting. Some sources claim that Parmenio advised against a Macedonian assault in such difficult terrain, but Alexander answered that he would be ashamed of himself "if a little trickle of water like this were too much." Plutarch writes that the king simply plunged into the river with 13 squadrons of cavalry. Diodorus, however, reports that Alexander took his infantry downstream and led them across by cover of darkness.

General Parmenio had been given command of the army's left wing with his son Philotas on the far right. Alexander himself—conspicuous in his double white-plumed helmet—was at the head of the Companion Cavalry. Ranged against them were 20,000 Persian cavalry. Despite their superior numbers, in strengthening their left wing to oppose Alexander's position on the right, the Persians had fatally weakened their own center.

Following an initial silence, Alexander launched the attack to the sound of trumpets and battle cries. The scout cavalry under Amyntas managed to pin down the Persian left wing, whereupon Alexander led the Companions into the left center of the enemy ranks. With reinforcements having made their way up the river bank, the Macedonians were soon fighting on equal terms, and their strict adherence to their battle plan won the day. Plutarch and Arrian state that the Macedonians lost relatively few men. In contrast, Persian casualties numbered 22,500—the death toll would have been even greater had the Macedonians been ordered to pursue the fleeing enemy. Instead, Alexander concentrated his efforts on the Persian army's 15,000 Greek mercenaries, whom he regarded as traitors—in a furious assault, most of them were cut down where they stood.

In the aftermath of the Battle of the Granicus, Alexander sent 2,000 prisoners to Macedonia as slaves. Three hundred Persian shields were dispatched to Athens as an offering to Athena, with the inscription,

The allied army was transported from Europe into Asia by a fleet of triremes (Greek war ships) and merchant vessels. The first to reach land, Alexander leapt from his ship in full armor and, hurling his spear ashore, declared that Asia was his.

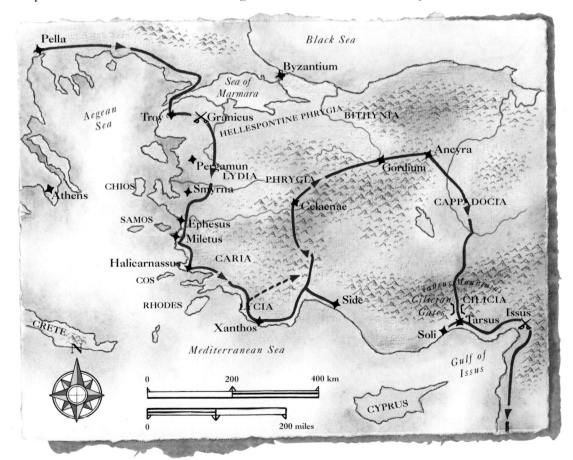

This detail of the 4th-century BCE "Alexander Sarcophagus" in Istanbul shows a Macedonian soldier seizing a fallen Persian by the hair before killing him. The scene gives a vivid impression of the fury of battle. In the midst of similar hand-to-hand combat during the Battle of the Granicus, the Persian nobleman Spithridates raised his scimitar ready to strike at Alexander's back. Black Cleitus (see page 91) saved his king's life by slicing off the Persian's arm.

"Alexander, son of Philip, and king of all the Greeks except the Spartans, gives these offerings taken from the foreigners who live in Asia."

News of the Macedonian victory traveled fast. As Alexander's army marched south through Asia Minor toward the strategic fortress of Sardis in Lydia, all the towns along the route surrendered to them. Alexander was welcomed everywhere as a great liberator. He wisely installed democracies in the cities he freed from Persian rule, exempted them from tribute payments, and left local laws untouched—he was creating a string of outposts on whom he would be able to rely for support in future. After crushing a rebellion at Miletus, most of the coast was in Macedonian hands—the Persian navy was fast becoming obsolete. Alexander decided to disband his own smaller fleet to save funds, keeping only 20 Athenian ships to transport siege engines. The Greeks took the last remaining Persian naval stronghold of Halicarnassus in Caria in the fall of 334BCE. Alexander returned the former queen of Caria, Ada, to her throne. She had supported the king since his arrival in Asia and even went on to adopt him as her son—thereafter, Alexander always addressed her as "mother."

With winter approaching, Alexander sent all his newly married troops home to their wives in Macedonia with orders to join up with the main army again the following spring. After securing the Lydian coast and Pamphylia against any further Persian naval interference, he turned his attention to Phrygia, which he took after stiff resistance.

In 333BCE Alexander reached Gordium. That summer, he famously "untied" the Gordian Knot by slashing through the rope with his sword. He was joined at Gordium by Parmenio and the rest of the army: the troops who had been sent home in the fall and more than 3,500 new recruits.

CHRONICLERS OF THE EXPEDITION

The most important record of Alexander's 11-year campaign was the king's own daily journal, which listed all royal business, including orders sent out, correspondence received, and army statistics. Composed by Alexander's chief private secretary, Eumenes of Cardia, this journal in effect comprised Macedonia's state records and as such was highly confidential.

It has been estimated that Alexander's journal must have stretched to at least 20 volumes. After the king's death, Ptolemy took Alexander's body and personal possessions to Egypt. These must have included the royal journal, which Ptolemy presumably used when writing his history of Alexander's life. Although, like the journal, Ptolemy's eye-witness account published in 285BCE is now lost, it was referred to by Arrian of Nicomedeia almost five centuries later. It is Arrian's abbreviated version of Ptolemy which remains the most reliable account of Alexander's life and campaigns.

Alexander employed Aristotle's nephew Callisthenes to act as the official campaign historian. Callisthenes' work, only fragments of which survive, was published in instalments from 332BCE until his death in 327BCE. Other accounts written on campaign include that of the Macedonian Companion Marsyas of Pella (whose writing formed the basis of the Roman historian Curtius' knowledge). Some of the specialists who kept a log included the engineer Aristobulos of Phocis and the naval commander Nearchus. Chares wrote about life at court and Onesicitus of the marvels he had seen in India.

333BCE

VICTORY AT ISSUS

With the army infused with new recruits and men fresh after a winter at home, orders were given to march south from Gordium across Anatolia. In summer 333BCE, Alexander and his army crossed the Taurus Mountains through the undefended pass known as the "Cilician Gates" and descended onto the fertile plain below. In September, while still recovering from a major bout of fever during which doctors had feared for his life, Alexander undertook a short campaign to subdue the Cilicians occupying the foothills. He then marched east to Malus, where he received a dispatch containing much-awaited news. Darius had marched west and was now only two days away, encamped to the east of the Syrian Gates at Sochi. At last, Alexander was about to meet the Great King in battle.

Darius had arrived from Babylon with an army estimated by Ptolemy to comprise 600,000 men, thereby outnumbering the Greek army ten to one. The Persians had also secured the perfect strategic field position to stage the battle—the sweeping plains of Syria—enabling Darius to use his massive numerical advantage to best effect.

In only two days Alexander marched 70 miles (110 kilometers) to Myriandrus on the shores of the Gulf of Issus, but it was too late. Darius had already gone—unaware that Alexander had been ill, the Persian king had believed that his adversary was simply afraid to face him. Assuming Alexander was still in Cilicia, Darius ordered his army northward. The two armies passed each other on either side of the Amanus Mountains.

Arriving in the Bay of Issus in Alexander's wake, the Persians came across a Greek field hospital, where they killed most of the wounded and maimed the rest. A few survivors got away by boat and informed

OVERLEAF The Battle of Issus is depicted in a Roman copy of a 4th-century BCE Greek painting. A terrified Darius is shown about to take flight as Alexander leads the charge against the Persian army.

Alexander of what had happened. Furious, the Macedonian leader turned his force around and marched back up the coast to face Darius.

At dawn the next day Alexander marched his army out onto the narrow plain between the sea and the mountains, a setting that would nullify the Persians' numerical advantage. On that November morning it soon became obvious that the main attack would come from the Persian right, made up of 10,000 élite cavalry located next to the sea.

As the two armies faced each other across the Payas river, Alexander rode up and down the lines lifting morale by picking out individuals to praise their previous feats of bravery. Having assessed the enemy, he realized that Darius had placed his untrained infantry under the protection of archers on the right. Leading the Companions, Alexander charged into the river astride Bucephalas and up the opposite bank. The Persian archers fired an ineffective volley, panicked, and ran into their own infantry. In the ensuing chaos the Persian left flank collapsed. Casualties piled up as

This painting by Albrecht Altdorfer (1480–1538) is entitled *The Battle of Alexander*. The piece is thought to be a portrayal of the vast scale and terrible ferocity of the fateful Battle of Issus, based on descriptions that appear in various classical accounts of the campaigns of Alexander the Great.

fierce fighting engulfed both the center and the right. Alexander then made for Darius' position behind the Greek mercenary line, where the Great King stood in his war chariot surrounded by his élite bodyguard. As Alexander approached, Darius lost his nerve and fled the field, leaving his troops in disarray. The Greeks had triumphed.

Although Alexander had been wounded by a sword thrust, he visited his men on the day after their victory, comparing wounds and stories, before burying the dead with full honors. He also inherited Darius' tent filled with his abandoned treasures, including, most priceless of all, the Great King's family.

332BCE

THE SIEGE OF THE ISLAND CITY

Alexander and his army now advanced down the coast through Phoenicia, resisting the lure of a rapid assault against Darius to the east. Among the Phoenician cities to welcome the Macedonians were Byblos and Sidon. Beyond them lay Tyre, whose inhabitants dispatched an envoy expressing compliance with Alexander's wishes. Alexander announced his intention to sacrifice to the god Heracles (Tyrian Melcarth) within the city, knowing that this would test the Tyrians' new-found loyalty. The Tyrians promptly retorted that such a sacrifice was the exclusive prerogative of Tyrian kings. Alexander, who had foreseen this public insult, prepared for a siege—he was about to demonstrate his true military genius for the first time.

Tyre stood on an island 800 yards (730 meters) off the coast. Its seemingly impregnable fortifications were more than 150 feet (45 meters) high. Lacking reliable naval support, the Macedonians' only option was a time-consuming one—they would have to build a causeway to bridge the divide. This was at best a daunting task, but Alexander calculated that the basic raw materials required for such a causeway were close at hand—the walls of Old Tyre would provide the stone, and the nearby slopes of Mount Lebanon the timber. In January 332BCE, the Thessalian engineer Diades began the construction of the causeway, using thousands of local villagers as his workforce. The project advanced satisfactorily until it reached deeper water, where Tyrian ships began to attack by sea. Alexander responded by widening the causeway, enabling him to bring forward his 150-foot (45-meter) tall siege machines to defend the workers.

Six months into the causeway project, the 120-strong Cypriot fleet arrived in Sidon, having rebelled against Persian rule. Alexander's fleet,

which had also recently been boosted by 100 Phoenician ships from Arad, Byblos, and Sidon, was now much larger than that of the Tyrian navy.

At the sight of the new Macedonian fleet approaching, the Tyrians hastily blockaded their harbor. The Macedonians attacked Tyre on several fronts, with the naval assault pivotal. However, the Tyrians' ingenuity and determination (see right) enabled them to survive continuous naval blockading and battering for more than three months. Having seen countless numbers of men die in their attempts to bridge the walls of Tyre, in early July Alexander himself finally led his veteran troops over the walls and into the city, as the Cypriot and Phoenician fleets simultaneously forced the harbor boom. The Tyrians, sensing defeat, fled from the walls.

Six thousand Tyrians were killed and 30,000 enslaved—a heavy cost for defying Alexander. Angered by the Tyrians' murder of Macedonian envoys sent to offer peace in return for surrender before the start of the siege, and frustrated by the long, arduous campaign, the Macedonians also crucified 2,000 Tyrian fighters along the seashore.

With the Persian navy in ruins, Darius sent Alexander a second envoy (an earlier proposal of an alliance in exchange for the safe return of the Persian royal family had been angrily turned down). The new envoy bore a peace treaty offering Alexander all of Asia Minor west of the Euphrates, the hand of the Great King's daughter in marriage, and 10,000 talents to safeguard the Persian royal family. Alexander instantly rejected the offer, stating that he already held the countries of Asia Minor and their treasures, and could marry Darius' daughter with or without her father's permission.

The siege of a 4th-century BCE city is depicted on the Xanthos Neried frieze: while defenders prepare to throw missiles, a female inhabitant looks on in terror. During the battle that ended their siege of Tyre, the Macedonians used torsion catapults to hurl rocks at the city walls, bow-type catapults to pierce armor, ships with battering rams, and siege towers with drawbridges. At the height of the battle, the Tyrians produced their secret weapon—red-hot sand poured from the top of the walls, which drove many Macedonians to hurl themselves into the sea in a desperate attempt to relieve their burns.

—— 332–331BCE ——

HAIL TO THE PHARAOH

With the whole of Asia Minor now his, Alexander was free to pursue the Persians east into their own heartlands. However, knowing that it would take Darius at least a year to muster a new army after his defeat at Issus (see page 47), Alexander chose instead to go south to Egypt. Although often regarded by later historians as little more than an eccentric diversion, Alexander's six-month Egyptian sojourn was essential to his future plans—he required a strong coastal base for both strategic and commercial purposes. However, the founding of the city of Alexandria was not the only legacy of the young king's time in Egypt. His stay there marked a major psychological turning-point in his life, for it was in Egypt that he became convinced of his own invincibility and divinity.

With Hephaestion's naval reinforcements following his progress down the coast, Alexander covered the hazardous 130 miles (210 kilometers) from Gaza—where he had successfully overcome a stand against him—to Pelusium in a week, arriving in late October. Although Pelusium was heavily fortified, Egypt's Persian satrap (governor), Mazaces, had no armed forces and no prospect of receiving any assistance following Darius' swift departure after the Battle of Issus. The Macedonian king's reputation went before him, and Mazaces greeted Alexander without offering any resistance, even handing over the treasury's 800 talents and "all the royal furniture" to the Macedonians.

After installing a garrison at this key defensive site, Alexander ordered his fleet to sail up the Nile to the traditional capital of Memphis (Inebhedj) at the apex of the Delta. The king himself would arrive by land at the head of his troops. The ancient religious site of Heliopolis (Iunu), with its vast white temples and towering obelisks, must have amazed the Macedonian troops and their 24-year-old leader as they marched past it on their journey southward. Olympias had regaled her young son with tales of Egyptian gods, and of a land steeped in ritual, where priests wielded enormous power from within awe-inspiring temples—these images would have made an indelible impression on the religiously-minded Alexander. Having passed by the great pyramids of Giza (which at that time were still clad in shining white limestone), Alexander finally entered Memphis, where he received a genuinely rapturous welcome.

For almost 200 years, Egypt had been occupied by Persia. Having assumed the Egyptian crown by right of conquest, the Persian king ruled *in absentia* through a satrap, exploited Egypt's vast grain reserves, and taxed its people heavily. The Persians, who showed little respect for ancient Egyptian traditions, were deeply unpopular—the Egyptians had rebelled so often that some parts of the country remained virtually independent. Alexander was therefore hailed as a savior and liberator by the Egyptian people and ruling classes alike, and was offered the

The Egyptian hieroglyphs on this 4th-century BCE tablet spell out phonetically the name "Aleksandros."

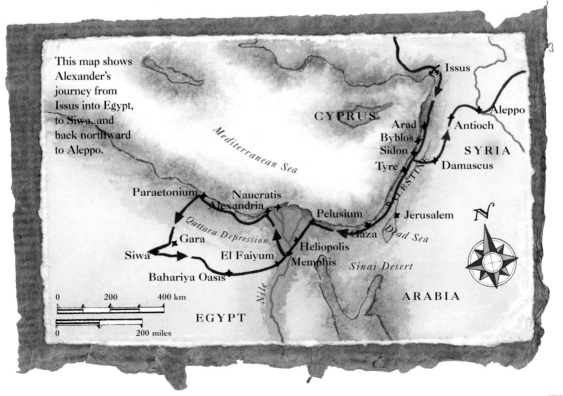

This map shows Alexander's journey from Issus into Egypt, to Siwa, and back northward to Aleppo.

Detail of a monumental statue of Alexander the Great from Luxor. The king is portrayed wearing the traditional royal headcloth (*nemes*) of the Egyptian pharaoh, with his characteristic curls shown in Greek style at the forehead. The statue was probably made during Alexander's reign.

double crown of Upper and Lower Egypt. He was anointed as pharaoh in Memphis on 14 November 332BCE.

At the Memphite necropolis of Sakkara, the new pharaoh offered sacrifices to the Apis bull, cult animal of the creator god Ptah. Alexander then held Greek-style games and literary contests in which performers from all over the Greek world took part in a multi-cultural extravaganza. These events mark the beginnings of Hellenism in their blending of Greek practices and local traditions. Egypt and Greece would successfully co-exist for the next three centuries.

For two months Alexander resided in the royal palace at Memphis. Although exaggerated for propaganda purposes, the Persians' disregard for Egyptian religious traditions had decreased the clergy's powers and so the priesthood joined enthusiastically with the populace to hail Alexander as pharaoh. As for the Macedonian leader, he remembered Plato's words, "In Egypt it is not possible for a king to rule without the priests' support." He upheld all the traditional practices expected of a pharaoh, from making the correct offerings to restoring and rebuilding Egypt's religious centers, including the southern temples of Luxor and Karnak. On the walls of the temple of Luxor, Alexander is repeatedly depicted in traditional pharaonic regalia in the company of Egypt's supreme deity Amun, king of the gods. Just like his royal predecessors, Alexander is also regularly portrayed with the rams' horns associated with Amun curling through his hair (see page 58). Alexander's image was replicated throughout Egypt in both monumental statuary and delicate relief. His portraits are accompanied by the hieroglyphic equivalent of his Greek name, enclosed by a royal cartouche: "Horus, strong ruler, he who seizes the lands of the foreigners, beloved of Amun and the chosen one of Ra, meryamun setepenra Aleksandros."

Alexander spent much of his time in Memphis studying Egyptian laws, customs, and philosophy in the company of his closest Companions, including Hephaestion, Craterus, and Ptolemy. The latter's experience in Egypt would stand him in good stead when he later became a pharaoh himself (see page 155).

Alexander left Memphis in January 331BCE and sailed down the western branch of the Nile to inspect the Greek trading colony of Naucratis. Its land-bound position offered no scope for development, so the king pressed on toward the Egyptian fort of Rhacotis (referred to by both Herodotus and Thucydides). The fort stood close to Lake Mareotis, where a narrow ridge divides its waters from the sea opposite the island of Pharos. This shore, with its sheltered natural harbor was to be the site of Alexandria, gateway between Egypt and the Mediterranean, and the first of numerous cities to bear the conqueror's name (see pages 60–61).

THE DIVINE RULER

The culmination of the ancient ceremony during which Alexander was crowned as pharaoh came when the Egyptian high priests named their new ruler "son of the gods." This title had a profound affect on the young Macedonian king.

Always a devout man, Alexander never had any difficulty worshiping foreign deities as aspects of his own gods, and he quickly equated the Greek god Zeus with the Egyptian god Amun (Libyan Ammon). The title "son of the gods" must have reminded Alexander of Olympias' claim that he was really the son of Zeus (see page 15). In a world in which the gods were perceived as living entities and were considered a part of everyday life, Alexander now began to believe his own propaganda concerning his divinity. This conviction was to influence his behavior for the rest of his life.

At the temple of Khnum, Elephantine, Alexander IV, the son of Alexander the Great, is portrayed in the same way as his illustrious father, in the traditional pharaonic regalia of a son of the gods.

331BCE

ORACLE IN THE DESERT

Having chosen the site of Alexandria on the Mediterranean shores of the Nile delta (see page 53), Alexander set out west along the coastal road to Paraetonium (modern Mersa Matruh) in late January 331BCE, leaving the main body of his army in Egypt. The king's military escort included his friends and Companions together with local guides. As they advanced 200 miles (320 kilometers) along the coast toward Libya, the Macedonians received envoys from the Greek colony of Cyrene offering their allegiance.

Alexander then turned south to follow the ancient caravan route through the northern Sahara, which connected the Mediterranean coastline to central Africa via the all-important network of oases. The major oasis at Siwa was also home to the renowned oracle of the god Amun (Libyan Ammon) described in Herodotus' Histories (II.31–2), which Alexander, like many other famous men before him, intended to consult.

After a few days crossing the sands, the party ran out of water and were only saved by a sudden violent rainstorm, interpreted by the expedition's historian Callisthenes as divine intervention. Their progress was then interrupted by one of the terrifying sandstorms that regularly sweep up from the south obliterating any recognizable landmarks. With the track indistinguishable from desert, and the landscape featureless as far as the eye could see, even the party's local guides were soon lost. However, disaster was averted when, according to ancient sources, two black ravens miraculously appeared. Alexander exhorted his colleagues to follow the birds, as he believed they had been sent by the gods to guide them. Callisthenes records that the ravens flew slowly so that the party could keep up, and even cawed loudly if their charges deviated from the correct

path. However, Ptolemy claims that two snakes guided the group, and while unsure which account to believe, Arrian confesses, "I have no doubt whatever that he [Alexander] had divine assistance of some kind." Plutarch later wrote of the king, "Fortune, by giving in to him on every occasion, had made his resolve unshakable and so he was able to overcome not only his enemies, but even places and seasons of the year."

When the exhausted travelers finally entered Siwa they must have been enchanted by the beauty of its lush, fertile oasis. Shady groves of palms and fruit trees bordered waters that gushed forth in abundance from subterranean springs.

Anxious to visit the oracle as soon as possible, Alexander went immediately to the temple of Amun, which was located on the high rock outcrop of Aghurmi. Plutarch says that, according to his sources, Alexander

The Siwa oasis today. Immense curiosity and excitement must have greeted Alexander's soldiers emerging here weary from the desert, at their head the first pharaoh ever to complete the dangerous journey.

DEPICTING THE SON OF AMUN

By Alexander's day, the worship of Amun had spread from the shrines of Egypt and Libya across the ancient world. In 333 BCE in Athens a temple of Amun had even been inaugurated in which the Egyptian Amun and Libyan Ammon were equated with the Greeks' supreme deity Zeus, king of the gods.

The Egyptian king of the gods Amun was often represented by his sacred animal the ram, and the characteristic horns were adopted by certain pharaohs as part of their royal regalia.

At the temple of Luxor, where Amenhotep III is depicted with the ram's horns, Alexander is also represented in the company of Amun. Thereafter, Alexander was frequently portrayed with the horns of Amun curling through his hair and, as his legend grew he became known as far afield as Iran as the "two-horned one."

This silver *tetradrachm* of Lysimachus (360–281 BCE)—King of Thrace after Alexander's death—was issued by the Pergamum mint and depicts Alexander wearing the royal diadem and the ram's horns of Amun.

was met by the Siwan high priest who greeted him with the words, "*O, paidion*," ("Oh, my son"), but mispronounced the Greek as "*O, pai dios*," meaning "Oh, son of god," much to Alexander's delight and amazement. His small party waited in the temple forecourt. One of the Macedonians asked the oracle whether they might give their king divine honors, to which the reply came, "This would please Amun." Then, in his capacity as pharaoh and high priest of all the gods, Alexander was led into the scented darkness of the inner sanctuary to put his secret questions to the mighty god himself.

When he finally reappeared in the daylight, Alexander would say only he had been given "the answer his heart desired." It is likely that the main subject discussed had been the nature of his divine paternity, since he was adamant that the only other person he would tell these "secret prophecies" to would be his mother, on his return to Macedonia. Plutarch claims that Alexander also asked whether his father's murder had been avenged, whereupon "the high priest asked him to choose his words more carefully, for his father was not a mortal." He may also have sought divine

approval for his new Egyptian city. Whatever Alexander's questions had been, he was sufficiently satisfied with the answers to present magnificent offerings to the oracle, and for the rest of his life he sent frequent gifts to its priests, together with more questions. Alexander, whose faith in oracles was unshakeable, was always particularly eager to receive answers from Siwa. He would also act on the oracle's advice, whether it suited his purpose or not. When Hephaestion died, for example (see pages 148–9), Alexander's envoys returned from Siwa with the news that Amun had refused the king's request that Hephaestion be worshiped as a god, but had decreed that he could be honored as a divine hero.

According to Ptolemy, Alexander then returned to the Nile Valley along the more direct 300-mile (480-kilometer) route across the Qattara Depression. On his arrival in Memphis 18 days later, he made sacrifices to Zeus-Amun, held a great parade of troops, and received 500 Greek mercenaries and 400 Thessalian cavalry sent by Antipater.

The pharaoh then made arrangements for the governing of Egypt in his absence. Arrian writes that Alexander had been deeply impressed by Egypt, "and the general strength of the country, but the fact this had been greater than he expected, induced him to divide the control of it between a number of his officers, as too unsafe to put it all in the hands of one man." Following Aristotle's advice that a king must hold an even balance between all parties, Alexander appointed a combination of Egyptians, Macedonians, and Persians to rule Egypt along traditional lines. The Macedonian Cleomenes was installed as the new governor of Egypt, but Alexander wisely utilized the experience of the deposed Persian satrap Mazaces, keeping him on as part of the new administration.

While he was in Memphis, Alexander received the welcome news that Cyprus, Rhodes, and Phoenicia, and the Aegean islands of Tenedos, Lesbos, Cos, and Chios had all come over to his side. When their former pro-Persian leaders were delivered to him for judgment, Alexander dispatched them south to the Greek garrison at Aswan, accompanied by Callisthenes, who was instructed to investigate Aristotle's theory that the annual Nile flood was a result of rains to the south.

Alexander left Egypt in mid-April 331BCE a changed man, and although he would never return alive to see the city he had founded, it would eventually become his final resting place (see pages 158–9).

CITIES OF ALEXANDER

Alexander the Great, the conqueror of countless cities, also created as many as 70 new ones. Founded as part of his policy of "conquest through civilization," each settlement was designed along Greek lines with the help of the king's architects, town planners, and technical advisors. The vast network of new towns that Alexander left was the key to the Hellenization of the huge area he had conquered. This Hellenization was to continue for hundreds of years after the king's death (see pages 160–65).

Alexander named many of his new settlements after himself, although some bore the names of departed companions, including his horse Bucephalas (see page 117). Some new settlements were memorials: after the Battle of Gaugamela, Alexander renamed the hill Tell Gomel "Nikatorion," meaning

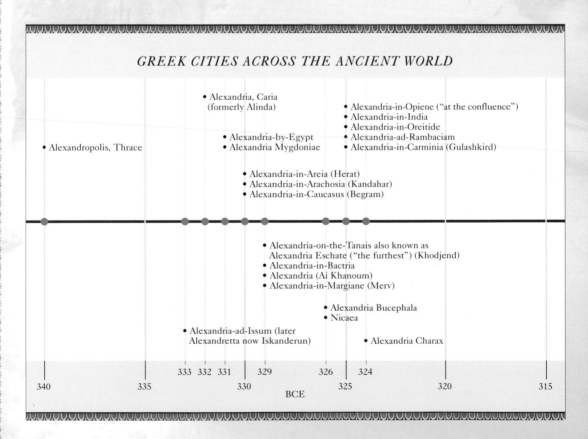

GREEK CITIES ACROSS THE ANCIENT WORLD

- Alexandria, Caria (formerly Alinda)
- Alexandria-in-Opiene ("at the confluence")
- Alexandria-in-India
- Alexandria-in-Oreitide
- Alexandria-by-Egypt
- Alexandria-ad-Rambaciam
- Alexandria Mygdoniae
- Alexandria-in-Carminia (Gulashkird)
- Alexandropolis, Thrace
- Alexandria-in-Areia (Herat)
- Alexandria-in-Arachosia (Kandahar)
- Alexandria-in-Caucasus (Begram)
- Alexandria-on-the-Tanais also known as Alexandria Eschate ("the furthest") (Khodjend)
- Alexandria-in-Bactria
- Alexandria (Ai Khanoum)
- Alexandria-in-Margiane (Merv)
- Alexandria Bucephala
- Nicaea
- Alexandria-ad-Issum (later Alexandretta now Iskanderun)
- Alexandria Charax

333 332 331 · 329 · 326 · 324

340 · 335 · 330 · 325 · 320 · 315

BCE

"Mountain of Victory." Other cities, such as Alexandria Charax between the Tigris and Eulaeus rivers, were designed in part to become great commercial centers, creating a new market place for the Mediterranean world. However, like Alexandria and Nicaea in Bactria, most of the cities Alexander founded were defensive outposts, occupying strategic positions and populated with a mixture of Macedonians and native people.

Alexandria on the coast of the Nile Delta (see page 53) was to prove the most enduring of all the cities created by Alexander—a vibrant and lasting legacy to his vision of a new world. His choice of the site, and his very personal involvement in the city's design is typical of the energy he devoted to the founding of his namesakes. As Arrian writes, the king "himself designed the general layout of the town, indicating the position of the market place and the temples ... and the exact limits of the defenses." Alexander even planned the site of the royal palace, and worked out a complex system of underground drains.

However, as its name implies, Alexandria-by-Egypt was never fully integrated into Egyptian culture. It remained a flourishing Greek city, populated by Greek settlers, members of the Egyptian élite, and a large Jewish community, ruled over by a Macedonian monarchy. By 300BCE, it was a truly cosmopolitan melting pot—into Alexandria's grand Mediterranean harbor flowed an endless stream of new people, goods, and ideas.

CHAPTER THREE

THE GREAT KING

331–327BCE

This majestic winged bull appears on a detail of glazed tiles from the
Achaemenid royal palace at Susa, where the victorious Alexander
ascended the throne of the Persian Great King (see page 69).

<hr />

331BCE

DARIUS FLEES EAST

In preparation for his renewed offensive against Persia, Alexander led his army out of Egypt and back to Tyre (see pages 50–51). In the two years since the Battle of Issus, he had resisted chasing after Darius, who was now 700 miles (1,125 kilometers) to the east in Babylon. Instead, Alexander had neutralized the Persian fleet and reinforced his own lines of communication. He had given the Persians plenty of time in which to assemble a new army, which he then intended to defeat once and for all. The Battle of Gaugamela was to provide that much-awaited opportunity.

In this detail from the Issus Mosaic (see pages 48–9) a frightened Darius is portrayed facing Alexander before fleeing the Battle of Issus. The encounter at Gaugamela was to be equally humiliating for the Persian king.

Having marched in the summer heat from Tyre to Nisibis in Assyria, the Macedonian army turned south toward Arbela. Alexander, who learned that the Persians were waiting northwest of Arbela at Gaugamela, pitched camp seven miles (11 kilometers) away. At daybreak on 1 October, the Macedonian king addressed his men, as he always did, lifting their spirits by telling them that, despite their superior numbers, the enemy had neither the heart nor the discipline for warfare. This battle, Alexander told his soldiers, was for the whole of Asia.

Lined up on the battlefield at Gaugamela were Darius' 100,000 infantry and 40,000 cavalry, together with scythed chariots and Indian war elephants. Alexander commanded just 40,000 infantry and 7,000 cavalry. To counteract such enormous numbers, his strategy was similar to that at the Battle of Issus—to draw as many of the enemy as possible away from the center, which he would then attack. Parmenio's cavalry took the left flank. The

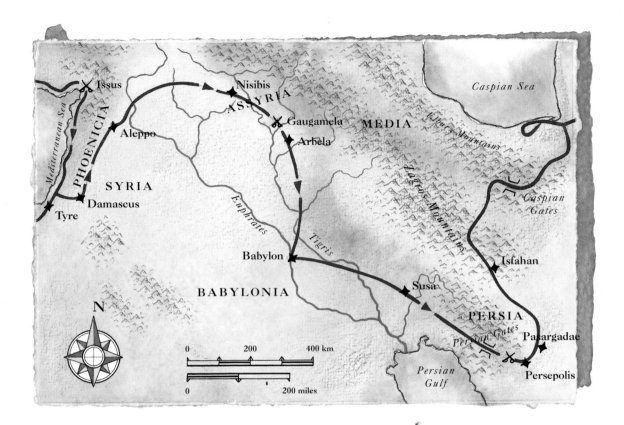

Macedonian phalanx was at the center, opposite Darius' cavalry and infantry. Alexander fought on the right, leading the Companion Cavalry opposite the Great King's cousin Bessus. With his army almost completely surrounded at one point, Alexander was relying on his men on the flanks to create a break in Persian lines; when this happened he was ready. Changing horses to allow 24-year-old Bucephalas to share in his greatest triumph, Alexander led the Companions' charge straight at Darius.

In the hand-to-hand fighting, 60 Companions were killed or injured as the Persian Royal Guards, or "Immortals," fought bravely to the death to defend their king. Alexander's spear narrowly missed Darius, killing the charioteer beside him; in fear of his life, the Great King fled. Realizing Darius had deserted them, the Persians began to retreat. With victory his, Alexander sped off southeast, hoping to catch up with Darius, but the latter had escaped across the Taurus Mountains, accompanied by Bessus.

Alexander, King of Macedon, Hegemon of Greece, Overlord of Asia Minor, and Pharaoh of Egypt was now proclaimed Great King and ruler of Asia by right of conquest. Yet Darius himself had once more eluded him.

From Tyre, the Macedonian army marched to the Euphrates river, which they crossed in early August. Darius expected Alexander to advance on Babylon, but instead—as the above map shows—he turned northward into Assyria (now northern Iraq), thus luring the Persians away from the optimum battle conditions they had secured on Babylon's open plains.

331BCE

THE PALACE OF NEBUCHADNEZZAR

Alexander was now the ruler of Asia. With the rich heartlands of Babylon, Susa, and Persepolis lying largely undefended in the east, he decided against taking his army over the difficult terrain of the Taurus Mountain passes in pursuit of Darius. Instead, he chose to concentrate his efforts at the center of the empire he had inherited. On 2 October, Alexander left Arbela and marched south along the Royal Road to Babylon. At the entrance to the fabled city, Darius' satrap Mazaeus, accompanied by his sons, was waiting to greet the conqueror. Assuring the Macedonians of a peaceful welcome, Mazaeus handed over Babylon and its fabulous treasure, and the Babylonian people came out in force—just as the Egyptians had done in Memphis—to greet Alexander as "Liberator."

Alexander's first act on entering Babylon was to meet with the city's priesthood, the Chaldaeans. He then ordered the restoration of the ancient temples, which had been destroyed on the orders of the Persian king Xerxes after Babylon's failed rebellion in 482BCE. Surviving contemporary cuneiform records, known as the "Alexander Tablets," refer to the financial transactions involved in the king's temple restoration program.

Before taking up residence at the spectacular, 600-roomed south palace built in the sixth century BCE by King Nebuchadnezzar, Alexander paid homage at the shrine of Bel (Marduk). There, like the rulers of Babylon before him, he approached the god's statue and clasped its hands to receive divine powers, before offering sacrifices to Bel according to the priests instructions. By honoring native traditions in this way, Alexander earned the eternal gratitude of Babylon's priests and people. As in Egypt, his policy of reviving customs ignored during the two centuries of Persian rule succeeded in making him a far more acceptable ruler, in the eyes of his subjects, than his predecessors had been.

Once the temple restoration program was in place, Alexander began to organize Babylon's administration. In a pattern that was to be repeated throughout his empire, he kept the Persian governor in his post but, as a safeguard, also appointed Greeks to key administrative positions. Babylon's traditional and highly efficient native bureaucracy remained largely intact, serving the needs of a cosmopolitan population made up of Babylonians, Iranians, Arabs, Indians, and Jews.

Having been rewarded from the royal treasury, Alexander's soldiers

As Alexander's procession passed through Babylon's Ishtar Gate to the great palace, the Babylonians danced and threw rose-petals before their new king's golden chariot. Babylon was the most imposing city in the ancient world: its great crenellated outer walls were wide enough at the top to allow two four-horse chariots to pass alongside each other with ease, and the inner walls were faced with glittering blue and gold enamel tiles. Irrigation canals intersected the city streets and allowed vegetation to flourish along the walkways and stone terraces which made up the famous "Hanging Gardens." This half-size model of the 6th-century BCE Ishtar Gate was built at the site in Iraq in the 20th century CE.

COINS FOR A NEW EMPIRE

The first coins were minted in the mid-seventh century BCE by the Greeks of Lydia. Although in his day many people still relied on a barter economy, Alexander understood the importance of coinage in international transactions, and that coins provided the only practical way to pay his enormous standing army.

Alexander brought Macedonia in line with the rest of the eastern Mediterranean by adopting the widely-used Attic standard. Amphipolis became the Macedonians' most prolific mint, producing more than 13 million silver *tetradrachmae* for the regions of Thrace and Asia Minor over an 18-year period, beginning ca. 334BCE.

As his empire grew, Alexander recognized the need for a source of coin production nearer his center of operations in the Persian heartlands of Babylon and Susa. The treasure he had inherited from King Darius included 40,000–50,000 silver talents and 9,000 darics in gold ingots. (In 1931, it was calculated that in total this treasure would be worth £14 million, or US$63 million by the standards of the day.) Alexander had become the richest man on earth.

He founded a royal mint in Babylon where the ingots were melted down in vast numbers to produce hand-punched coins of standard weight and value. The Babylonian mint became the second-most prolific of the ancient world after Amphipolis. In creating it, Alexander single-handedly changed the entire

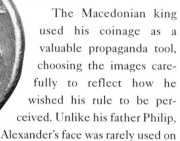

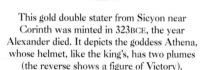

This gold double stater from Sicyon near Corinth was minted in 323BCE, the year Alexander died. It depicts the goddess Athena, whose helmet, like the king's, has two plumes (the reverse shows a figure of Victory).

economy of Asia—trade flourished as it had never done before.

The coins produced in Babylon were chiefly needed to pay Alexander's soldiers their often generous wages. (As a reward for their victory at Gaugamela in 331BCE Alexander gave each man 600 *drachmae*—the equivalent of a year's full pay.)

While he was in Babylon, Alexander also created a traveling treasury from which to pay his men on their future campaigns as he led them ever further east.

The Macedonian king used his coinage as a valuable propaganda tool, choosing the images carefully to reflect how he wished his rule to be perceived. Unlike his father Philip, Alexander's face was rarely used on his coins in his own lifetime. Instead, he chose images of the gods—the four used for his standard-issue coinage were Zeus, Amun, Heracles, and the Macedonian form of the war goddess, Athena Alcidemus. Alexander's coins also feature emblems of kingship, including the lion and the royal cap (*kyrbasia*) encircled with the purple ribbon (*mitra*).

It was only after his death that Alexander's face began to appear routinely on coinage. He is usually shown wearing appropriate headgear: his plumed helmet, lion skin, ram horns, or elephant hide. These devices were adopted by those keen to portray themselves as Alexander's true successors. Their coins are the only lasting legacy of many of those who sought to emulate him.

were housed in comfort and treated with great hospitality by the citizens of Babylon. Alexander, meanwhile, enjoyed five weeks of leisure, exploring the ancient city and relaxing in the luxurious Palace of Nebuchadnezzar where he was staying.

However, in late November, Alexander was on the move again. He entered the city of Susa, unopposed, in early December. The city's 200-year-old Winter Palace had 70-foot (20-meter) tall columns supporting its cedarwood roofs, beneath which Alexander ascended the golden throne of the deposed King of Kings, Darius. All the vast wealth of the palace was now his. Alexander delighted in taking possession of the treasures seized by Xerxes during the sack of Athens, including the archaic bronze statues of the Greek heroes Harmodias and Aristogeiton, which he sent back to their home on the Acropolis. The Persian kings had even filled their treasury with waters from the great Nile and Danube rivers, "as proof they were masters of the world"—a claim Alexander would soon exceed.

Susa's sumptuous palaces glistened with fabulous designs in glazed ceramic tiles of blue and gold, including this depiction of archers from the royal guard.

331–330BCE

AMBUSH AT THE GATES OF PERSIA

In mid-December, Alexander and his army left Susa to march 400 miles (650 kilometers) to Persepolis. To speed up his advance, he decided to divide his army at the point where the Royal Road branched southeast. He sent Parmenio and the heavy infantry and baggage train on the lower road across the plains through Shiraz. The king himself would lead a force of around 20,000 lightly-armed shock troops across the snowy, forested terrain of the Zagros Mountains and through the narrow, six-mile (10-kilometer) long pass of the Persian (or Susian) Gates on the very edge of the Persian homeland.

This head of Alexander, dated ca. 300BCE and copied from a bronze original, shows him wearing the lion headdress to symbolize both his courage and his relationship to his ancestor Heracles, who slayed the fabled Nemean lion and thereafter wore its skin.

The local satrap, Ariobarzanes, had built a defensive wall across the narrow pass with artillery hidden behind it, and had ranged 40,000 infantry and 700 cavalry along the ridges of the summit. In early January, outnumbered by more than two to one, the Macedonians mounted a direct assault. As they reached the narrowest section of the pass, the Persians unleashed a barrage of rocks, arrows, and javelins into the gorge, inflicting huge casualties on Alexander's men. In a hopeless position, the king sounded a temporary retreat, hastily backing off down the gorge to a clearing to the west.

Alexander was informed by a captive shepherd that the only route over the pass was a narrow, 12-mile (19-kilometer) footpath. Craterus and his men were left at the mouth of the gorge as a decoy. In the dead of night, the rest of the army were led through freezing blizzards across almost impassable terrain to the wide plateau of the summit at 7,500 feet (2,300 meters). It was agreed that three generals would lead their infantry brigades down to the plain of Ardakan, where they would bridge the Araxes

(Palvar) river for the army to cross and march to Persepolis. Meanwhile, Alexander took 4,000 men, supported by Ptolemy and 3,000 infantry reserves, to assemble at the back of the pass behind the Persian positions.

Before dawn, the king and his troops filed down into the gorge to arrive behind the Persian lines. At the agreed signal, Craterus and his men advanced from the entrance of the gorge as Alexander simultaneously launched his assault from behind. Ptolemy's infantry attacked down into the sides of the defenders. With no means of retreat, only a handful of Persians survived to escape on horseback with Ariobarzanes. The Macedonians had exacted their revenge for the previous day's slaughter.

Alexander and his army crossed swiftly into the province of Persis. The Royal Road to Persepolis lay wide open before them.

Detail of a battle scene between Greek and Persian soldiers from the Athenian temple of Athena Nike, built almost a century before Alexander finally led the Greeks into the heart of the Persian empire.

THE ROYAL ROUTINE

During Alexander's long campaigns, the king's typical day began with sacrifices to the gods before breakfast. Prior to a battle, he would discuss strategy with his War Council and engineers, but it was the administration of his ever-expanding empire that took up most of his time, despite the help of increasing numbers of advisors, officials, and translators. Alexander wrote large numbers of letters to the growing number of his governors and satraps, as well as to his many friends and to his family and the regent Antipater back in Macedonia.

In his moments of leisure, the king particularly enjoyed hunting, which kept him fit on campaign. He was also an avid reader, and his baggage always included a supply of books.

Passing through the cities he conquered, Alexander would take up temporary residence in their palaces. However, when on the march he lived under canvas alongside his men, albeit in a tent large enough to accommodate a royal audience or social gathering. His material needs were modest, and his tent was sparsely furnished. Each evening he bathed before having supper, always sharing the same food as his men. The king spent most evenings, when not receiving official guests, in the company of friends, talking and drinking late into the night, after which he would then bathe again and sleep, often for much of the following day if not on active service.

PERSEPOLIS: HEART OF AN EMPIRE

Darius I of Persia modeled much of Persepolis—the ruins of which are shown here—on plans drawn up by Cyrus the Great (who ruled 548–529BCE) for his capital Pasargadae, some 50 miles (80 kilometers) to the north. Within the foundations of the terrace at Persepolis, archeologists have found channels for a complex drainage and water system, suggesting that the complex was designed in detail before building work began.

The opulent city of Persepolis was Persia's holy city—the spiritual and ceremonial home of the great Achaemenid kings, chosen by the mighty god Ahura Mazda. Situated between the Araxes river and the Mountain of Mercy, part of the Kuh-i-Rahmat Mountain range, Persepolis was created on a grand scale by Darius I "the Great" (521–486BCE) ca. 520BCE, although its completion under Darius' successors Xerxes and Artaxerxes I took until ca. 460BCE. The Persians called this complex Parsa—it was the Greeks who later named it Persepolis, "city of the Persians."

Darius I's building inscriptions at Persepolis record that the site was given to the king by the god himself. "It is beautiful and contains good horses and good men, by the favor of Ahura Mazda and of me, Darius the king. It does not fear an enemy. By the favor of Ahura Mazda I built this place and Ahura Mazda commanded it be built. And so I built it to be secure and beautiful and fitting, exactly as I wished to do."

Persepolis was a majestic and imposing capital. Surrounded by huge, mud-brick defenses, with guard towers tiled in turquoise and white glaze, its main ceremonial structures were built on a great, stage-like terrace of limestone which rose to a height of 60 feet (18 meters).

Almost every surface was covered with superbly detailed raised relief images of the endless thousands of subjects who assembled each year to pay tribute to their mighty king, the focus of all activity. Repeated in regimented row after row, divided by lines of rosettes, the supplicants came from every part of the vast empire, dressed in their regional costumes—Persians resplendent in their flowing robes, Medes in coats and trousers, bejeweled with necklaces and golden earrings. Beards are styled in individual curls, with immaculately coiffed curled hairstyles topped with various forms of caps, turbans, and veils. All are flanked by the king's Immortal Guard (see illustration below), also dressed in splendid finery.

The complexities of Persian kingship and its religious ideologies were portrayed on every surface of Persepolis' royal core. Its temples were decorated with figures of Persian gods engaged in complex rituals, the king overcoming the demons of evil as fire altars blazed brightly in honor of Ahura Mazda, god of light. Inspired by the architecture of their Assyrian predecessors, gods and monsters were thought to provide a suitable backdrop for portraits of the Great King. Monumental stone figures of winged bulls and griffins guarded the entrances of the royal quarters, which lay behind huge bronze-covered doors decorated with rosettes.

Within the royal quarters were situated two grandiose, columned audience halls (*apadana*). The innovative 200-square-foot (18.5-square-meter) western audience chamber of Darius I, with its 36 columns reaching up 60 feet (18 meters), is said to have been large enough to accommodate up to 10,000 courtiers. Adjoining this to the east was the even larger hall of Xerxes, a 230-square-foot (21-square-meter) hall supported by no fewer than 100 columns and

On parade beneath a rosette border, members of the Persian Great King's royal bodyguard, complete with carefully dressed hairstyles and beards and long cloaks, march in endless procession along the walls of the ruined city of Persepolis.

decorated with relief images of Xerxes enthroned. The existence of two such halls may be explained by the later royal custom of using both a private and a public *apadana*: the former to receive close associates and special envoys or deal with personal or confidential matters, and the latter for carrying out the public business of issuing decrees and judging criminals.

Behind the hall of Xerxes lay the royal treasury, which contained the largest fortune in the world. The wealth of Persepolis was three times greater than that of Susa. Its treasuries spilled over with more than 120,000 talents. In addition, Darius III's personal quarters at Persepolis contained 8,000 talents and, in his bedroom, a bejeweled golden vine representing the Tree of Life and symbolizing the rightful government of the Achaemenid royal line under Ahura Mazda. By the standards of fifth-century BCE purchasing power, this combined treasure was worth 300 times the equivalent of the annual national income of the Athenian empire.

The walls of Persepolis' ceremonial center stood some 65 feet (20 meters) high, their standard mudbrick construction augmented with polished limestone doorways covered with blue and white glazed tiles, gilding, and panels of finest cedarwood affixed with golden nails. Cedar ceilings were supported by tall, fluted columns of marble or plastered and spiral-painted wood. The columns had bell-shaped bases and capitals carved into the shapes of lions, bulls, and mythical beasts, or palms and lotuses. The complex was accessed by a series of enormous stone staircases.

In spite of its repeated celebration of Ahura Mazda and the great kings, Persepolis' imposing splendor was the product of foreign craftsmanship. Nomadic people at heart, the Persians had no trained architects and relied instead upon skilled workers from the far reaches of their empire. Large numbers of captive Greek craftsmen were brought from Asia Minor to Persia to work. At Susa, Darius I had proclaimed in building inscriptions that "the stonecutters who wrought the stone were Ionians and Sardians," and in listing the unknown Telephanes alongside the greatest of Greek sculptors, the later Roman commentator Pliny remarks that the artist remained virtually unknown in the west, "because he devoted himself to the workshops of Xerxes and Darius." Yet there is hardly anything recognizably "western" about these works of art—because they were working for a static, hierarchical system, the foreign artists created suitably static, hierarchical images.

OVERLEAF The Apadana Staircase at the palace of Persepolis is lined with sculpted figures representing the arrival of humbled foreign ambassadors bearing gifts for the Great King of Persia.

CUSTOMS OF THE PERSIAN COURT

The Persian monarch was believed to be the living representative of the mighty god Ahura Mazda—he was surrounded by an aura of mystery and treated with great ceremony and respect.

Dressed in white and purple robes embroidered with gold, the Great King was transported in a gleaming chariot pulled by white horses, always with parasol and flywhisk bearers on hand. During court banquets, the king and his family dined hidden behind a veil. Attending nobles put aside some of the food from their table as an offering to him. On his accession, a fire was lit in the new monarch's honor and only extinguished at his death. His staff-bearers, should they outlive him, were killed beside his funeral pyre.

Access to this almost god-like king was strictly controlled and highly ritualized. A hundred years before Alexander's arrival in Persia, Herodotus had written that, when Persians of equal rank met in the street, "they kiss each other on the lips. Where one is a little the other's inferior, the kiss is given on the cheek; when the difference of rank is great, the inferior prostrates himself on the ground." All Persians, of course, were inferior to the king. Many of his subjects would have been expected to go down on their knees or fully prostrate themselves in the presence of their ruler.

A Mede bows before the Great King while bringing his hand to his lips, probably to blow a kiss. This was one of the respectful Persian gestures called *proskynesis* (obeisance) by the Greeks.

330BCE

A DYNASTY FALLS

With the Persian Gates behind him, Alexander crossed the Araxes river and sped on toward Persepolis. When he arrived in the ceremonial center of the Persian empire on 31 January 330BCE, the Macedonian leader received the formal surrender of the garrison commander Tiridates, together with the welcome news that all the palace strong rooms, containing 120,000 talents stored in solid bullion, were intact. Having held his men back at Babylon and Susa, Alexander now allowed them a day in which to plunder the wealthy residential quarters of Persepolis, "the most hateful city in Asia." The king himself would deal with the palaces of Darius I and Xerxes, the two invaders of Greece.

Biding his time in Persepolis, Alexander may have been expecting to be declared Great King and the "Chosen One of Ahura Mazda" at the culmination of the Great New Year Festival of Tribute. However, by late spring, it had become clear that this was not going to happen. The Persepolis clergy would not bestow the ritual kingship on an outsider, and the Macedonian ruler was clearly unacceptable to the local élite, who would always rally behind a native Persian and make Persepolis a center of nationalist rebellion.

To prevent this, Alexander seems to have decided to destroy the city that had failed to accept him—in May 330BCE, Persepolis was put to the torch. It is still unclear how this came about. Ptolemy's convincing eye-witness account of a premeditated act, recounted by Arrian, contrasts with the more sensationalized version (given by Diodorus, Curtius, and Plutarch), in which the fire was simply the accidental aftermath of a drunken party. As one of the guests at a party held in Xerxes' palace,

writes Plutarch, Ptolemy's mistress, Thais (an Athenian *hetaira*, or educated courtesan), suggested ending the party by "setting fire to the palace of Xerxes, who had laid Athens in ashes." Alexander is said to have jumped to his feet and led Thais and the dancing revelers in the throwing of burning torches. Whatever his true motivation, Alexander "quickly repented and gave orders for the fire to be put out." Yet for the Macedonians who watched the city become engulfed in flames this must have been the crowning moment of their campaign. With the war against Persia now over, they must have expected that soon they would be returning home in triumph. They were wrong. Poised between the worlds of east and west, Alexander saw that beyond Persepolis lay unchartered terrain, and it was into this unknown that he intended to lead his army.

   He resumed his pursuit of Darius in early June. Yet three days' march away from Ecbatana in Media, Alexander learned that Darius had retreated toward Bactra (Balkh) with the paltry remnants of the Persian army.

The terrible devastation that the Macedonians wreaked on Persepolis—which, as shown here, today lies in ruins—may be partly explained by an incident that had occurred as they approached the city. They met a group of escaping Greek slaves who had been so horribly mutilated by their Persian captors that Alexander is said to have wept at the sight.

—— 330BCE ——

SHAH OF SHAHS

In his retreat from Ecbatana toward Bactria, the Persian king was accompanied by his cousin Bessus, satrap of Bactria and commander of the Bactrian cavalry, and Nabarzanes the cavalry general and commander of the Persian guard. As it became clear that Darius had little chance of success, most of his men gradually deserted. With their forces and finances severely depleted, and Alexander's troops rapidly closing in, Nabarzanes claimed that the gods had foresaken Darius, and suggested that Bessus should take temporary command.

Soon after, the Great King was taken prisoner, and Bessus was hailed as king by his own Bactrian cavalry together with all the remaining Persian forces. Even Darius' bodyguards deserted him—only his eunuchs, including a young boy named Bagoas, stayed with their master.

Meanwhile, Alexander and his men covered a total of 400 miles (645 kilometers) in only 11 days, despite the fierce summer heat. They arrived at Rhagae (modern Rei, southeast of Tehran), only to learn that their royal quarry had already passed through the Caspian Gates (Kotal-e-Dochtar) and was pressing on east toward Afghanistan. Alexander was forced to rest his men for five days. Then followed another lightening advance; the troops passed through the Gates less than two days later, and marched on toward the great salt desert of Dasht-e-Kavir, south of the Elburz mountains. As Alexander rested in Choarene on the third day, the Babylonian nobleman Bagistanes and Mazaeus' son Antibelus—both deserters from Darius' army—arrived with news of the Great King's arrest.

Leaving most of his remaining troops under Craterus' command, Alexander rode on ahead at breakneck speed. On reaching the place where Darius had been arrested, he learned that the Great King had been bound in golden chains and was being carried in the back of a covered wagon. Bessus had had a head start, but a group of locals told Alexander of a shortcut through waterless, inhospitable terrain. Through the night, the Macedonian king led a small force of 500 horsemen along this dangerous route. At dawn, they finally sighted the fugitives' dust cloud near Shahrud. As Alexander closed in on the straggling band of Bactrians, most of Bessus' forces simply fled. Desperate to get away, Darius' captors tried to force him onto a horse, but the deposed Great King declared he would not leave with traitors—he preferred to stay and face Alexander. At this, the conspirators impaled Darius with their javelins. Leaving him fatally wounded in a bound and bloody heap, they fled into the desert.

When Alexander reached the spot where the wagon had been abandoned, he was met by the soldier who had discovered it and told, to his great disappointment, that he had arrived too late—Darius had died before the two kings could meet. Deeply moved, Alexander covered the body with his own cloak and gave orders for it to be embalmed and sent to the Persian queen mother Sisygambis, who was to give it a royal burial in Persepolis. It seems likely, given Alexander's treatment of Darius' family and the concessions he had outlined in letters to his vanquished foe, that, had Darius lived to acknowledge Alexander's supremacy as Lord of All Asia, he would have been reinstated as King of Persia and reunited with his family.

Despite Darius' demise, Alexander's new position as Shah of Shahs would only be completely secure when the usurper Bessus had been removed. Bessus, who had now taken the throne name Artaxerxes IV, was of royal blood and would always pose a threat. If he wished to be seen as Darius' true successor, Alexander had to keep up the chase until he could bring the murderers to justice.

This manuscript illustration was painted to accompany an edition of *Shahnama* by the 10th-century CE Iranian poet Firdowsi. The painting dates from ca. 1440–1445 and depicts Iskander (as Alexander was later known in the Eastern tradition) comforting the dying Darius. In fact, the Great King was already dead when Alexander reached him.

ROBES, CROWNS, AND PERFUMES

Dress was of great social significance in the ancient world. At a time when the vast majority of people were illiterate, clothing provided valuable information about an individual's status and allegiances, particularly among the élite. Highly skilled in the art of propaganda, Alexander the Great had a gift for manipulating his own image for political ends, especially through his choice of dress. According to the occasion, the king wore Macedonian state robes, dress armor, or foreign costume, and a wide variety of headwear, from hats to crowns (see box, opposite).

The court dress of Macedonian royal women included beautiful purple robes embroidered in gold, one of which was discovered in King Philip's tomb. Contemporary Macedonian jewelry displays superb craftsmanship: intricate goldwork is often set with precious gems. A fashion for Persian-type dress must also have emerged at Pella during Alexander's reign, inspired by the huge quantities of sumptuous embroidered textiles the king sent back to his mother and sister as he fought his way across Asia. (The textiles he recovered from Susa alone were worth more than 5,000 talents. They included more than 100 tons of purple cloth colored with a mixture of dye from the Gulf of Spetsae and honey, which, according to Plutarch, had kept their color fresh for almost 200 years.)

In Macedonia, male dress tended to be relatively sober and suited to the active lifestyle of the soldier. A Macedonian who had yet to kill a man wore a cord around his waist (Alexander discarded his while still a teenager). Noblemen were distinctive in their rich, purple cloaks. Given the militaristic nature of Macedonian society, armor was also an important form of dress. It was used not only as a protective measure, but also as a vital means of identification on the battlefield. The standard dress of a Macedonian Companion cavalryman comprised a short tunic, metal cuirass (to protect the chest and back), short leather or metal kilt, flowing cloak, sandals, and a metal helmet. Companion infantrymen wore similar dress of tunic, kilt, sandals, and a red cloak with the addition of metal leg greaves. Although only officers initially wore a metal cuirass, during Alexander's reign every

CROWNS AND CAPS, HATS AND HEADCLOTHS

Although he is most frequently depicted bareheaded with his unruly curls on full display, Alexander wore a great range of headwear throughout his life, from diadem to sun hat, as well as his charcteristic helmet and the emblematic headdresses of the gods.

The Pella lion-hunt mosaic (see page 19) shows Alexander wearing a *kausia*—the Macedonian broad-brimmed felt hat generally worn with a cloak. As a prince, he would also have worn a headband, and as king, a crown of gold leaves.

In the Luxor temple reliefs in Egypt, Alexander is shown wearing the traditional pharonic *nemes* head-cloth. At his coronation he would have received the white and red crowns of Upper and Lower Egypt. His later adoption of Persian royal dress included the traditional headwear of the Great King, the *kyrbasia* worn with the point erect and the purple-and-white *mitra* headband.

Alexander's war helmet was made of polished steel set with precious stones and two white plumes that made him conspicuous in battle. He is also sometimes portrayed wearing a helmet of lionskin (see right) or elephant hide, commemorating his victories in India.

This detail from a silver jar from Philip II's tomb shows the god Heracles wearing the skin of the Nemean lion he killed. This image was later adopted by Alexander.

infantryman was provided with this form of body protection.

Alexander's own distinctive armor is described in detail by Plutarch: "a tunic made in Sicily, which was belted at the waist, and over this a thickly quilted linen corset, which had been among the spoils captured at Issus. He also wore a cloak which was more ornate than the rest of his armor. It had been made by Helicon, an artist of earlier times, and presented to Alexander as a mark of honor by the city of Rhodes, and this too he was in the habit of wearing in battle." Alexander took pains to keep his armor in good condition and was quick to reprimand those less scrupulous.

The choice of armor could also be used to convey a political message. When Alexander took a set of armor said to have been used in the Trojan War from the temple of Athena in Troy, he was publicly declaring his intention of emulating the achievements of the Greek heroes who had so famously triumphed over their Asiatic rivals. Arrian reports that this highly symbolic set of armor acted as a talisman for the young king.

As he created his vast empire, Alexander adopted native costume where appropriate. In relief scenes at Luxor temple in Egypt, for example, the Macedonian leader has himself portrayed in the traditional costume of the Egyptian pharaoh (see also box, page 83).

Alexander also used costume for political purposes when he began to wear Persian clothes, a move which outraged many older Macedonians. Alexander appears to have adopted Persian dress around the same time he learned that the pretender Bessus had starting wearing the costume of a Great King, after proclaiming himself Artaxerxes IV (see page 86). Arrian states that Bessus "wore the royal mantle, and the *kyrbasia* (cap) with the point erect in royal fashion." However, Plutarch attributes this change in Alexander's image to somewhat different motives: "it was during a pause in campaign he first began to wear barbarian dress. He may have done this from a desire to adapt himself to local habits, because he undertood that the sharing of race and of custom is a great step towards softening men's hearts. Alternatively, this may have been an experiment which was aimed at introducing the obeisance among the Macedonians, the first stage being to accustom them to accepting changes in his own dress and way of life." Arrian, who strongly disapproved of Alexander's habit of wearing Persian dress, nevertheless concedes that it was "a matter of policy by which he hoped to bring the Eastern nations to feel that they had a king who was not wholly a foreigner."

During ritual events, both Philip and Alexander wore their dynasty's emblematic dress, the goatskin *aegis* (protective covering), which was associated with both Zeus and Athena.

Plutarch explains that Alexander adopted a style which was "a compromise between Persian and Median costume, more modest than the first and more stately than the second. At first he wore this only when he was in the company of barbarians or with his intimate friends indoors, but later he put it on when he was riding or giving audience in public." No doubt tutored in the exact nature of the Persian dress code by his close friends Artabazus, Oxathrates, and the eunuch Bagoas (see page 96), Alexander's variation of native costume seems to have included some form of long robe with a sash or girdle around the waist in the colors white and purple, and the *kyrbasia* with the point upward. It is also possible that the concealed heels of Persian shoes, rather than simple Greek sandals, may have given the Macedonian king the extra height he felt necessary to fulfill his role as successor of the six-foot (1.8-meter) tall Darius.

Alexander's attempts to persuade his Companions to wear white Persian cloaks with purple borders failed with traditionalists such as Cleitus and Craterus, who "clung to Macedonian customs." Hephaestion and others, however, were enthusiastic followers of the new trends.

Plutarch states that according to Aristoxenus, Alexander's clothing was permeated by his own natural odor, "the fresh, sweet fragrance of his skin," and that "his breath and the whole of his body gave off a distinctive fragrance." Unlike the average Macedonian soldier, Alexander's personal habits were fastidious, and he bathed on a daily basis. He had his own specialized staff (Athenophanes, Stephanus, and later Bagoas), "who waited on him whenever he bathed and anointed himself."

Whereas his father seems always to have worn a short, thick beard (see page 15), Alexander—unlike all previous Macedonian rulers—was clean shaven in the manner of southern Greece, a trend followed by the successors who tried to emulate him. Philip also seems to have kept his straight hair relatively short. In contrast, Alexander's fair hair was one of his trademarks, and is generally described and depicted as resembling a tousled mane, standing up a little over the forehead and falling into a center parting to frame his face in wavy, shoulder-length layers (see pages 106–109).

On the reverse of a silver *decadrachm* commemorating his triumph at the Battle of the Jhelum (see page 112), Alexander is depicted as the "King of Asia." He is shown wearing a helmet modeled on the *kyrbasia* royal Persian headdress.

330BCE

THE BETRAYAL OF PHILOTAS

Having moved at lightening speed in his attempt to save Darius, Alexander spent mid-July waiting for the main body of his troops to catch up with him. With the army back to full strength, the Macedonians marched into Hyrcania. They were met by the fugitive Persian Narbarzanes, whom Alexander pardoned for his part in Darius' murder, thus placing the blame firmly on Bessus. In Zadracarta (now Asterabad), Philip II's old Persian friend Artabazus also came to offer allegiance, along with his three sons. Another valuable new ally was Darius' brother Oxathres, who wanted to fight alongside Alexander to avenge his brother's murderers, and was made a Companion.

After a rousing speech quashing fresh rumors of an impending march home, Alexander led his army southeast in pursuit of the Great King's killer, who had proclaimed himself Artaxerxes IV.

At the Arian town of Susia (probably Meshed) Alexander reconfirmed the satrap Satibarzanes as governor of Aria and sent him back to his palace in Artacoana escorted by 40 Macedonian horsemen. On hearing reports that Bessus was expecting reinforcements from Scythia, Alexander set off at once for Bactria. However, some 75 miles (120 kilometers) south of Artacoana, Alexander was told that Satibarzanes had murdered his escorts, gone over to Bessus, and was arming the Arians for revolt. Furious, Alexander doubled back at breakneck speed and mercilessly put down the rebellion, although Satibarzanes himself managed to escape to Bactria.

Until this point, the Macedonian king had known only the rewards of power—tribute, loyalty, honor, and glory. However, he was about to be shocked by another betrayal, this time from within his own inner circle. Arriving in Phrada (Fara), Alexander learned of a plot against his life that

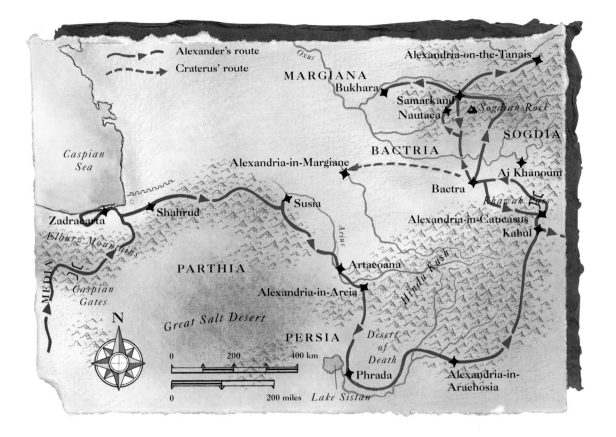

implicated Philotas—Parmenio's son and a friend of the king's since boyhood. Although events surrounding the incident remain unclear, it seems that, after receiving news of a plan to murder Alexander, Philotas failed to raise the alarm for two days. The plot was foiled when a page managed to get word of it to the king; the main conspirator was killed resisting arrest. Alexander's senior officers, many of them Philotas' enemies, agreed that the latter should be tried for treason. At his trial, Philotas denied all knowledge of the plot, saying that he had not considered the threat to be serious. However, Hephaestion, Coenus, and Craterus spoke out against him. A confession was extracted under torture, and Philotas was stoned to death according to Macedonian custom. To avoid a blood feud, it was crucial that news of his son's execution be kept from Parmenio, far away in Ecbatana. The king sent a message ordering senior soldiers to hand the general a letter supposedly from Philotas—in fact a forged message—informing him of the plot's success. Parmenio's smile on reading the news was their signal to strike, and he was killed in the grounds of his palace.

After putting down a rebellion in Aria in 330BCE, the Macedonians founded the town of Alexandria-in-Areia (Herat) to act as a military garrison for this potential trouble spot. As this map shows, they then continued their march through the infamous Desert of Death and then north toward the Hindu Kush.

329BCE

THE LAND OF
PROMETHEUS

In mid-winter, Macedonian troops had to be sent to quash a revolt when the Persian rebel Satibarzanes invaded Aria with a force supplied by Bessus. With the territories to the rear brought under control, Alexander rested his army for several months and established another settlement, Alexandria-in-Caucasus (near modern Begram). He then resumed his pursuit of the troublesome Bessus, who had already reached Bactria (Balkh); in spring 329BCE, the army set out to cross the Hindu Kush and into unchartered territory.

In order to cross the 11,600-foot (3,550-meter) high Khawak Pass—Alexander's chosen route through the mountains—the 32,000-strong army had to dispense with all wheeled transport and rely on pack animals. In his earlier advance through the same foothills, Bessus had undertaken a scorched-earth policy in the hope that Alexander's men would be so hungry and demoralized they would be forced to turn back. With all provisions exhausted by the second week, the starving Macedonian troops had no option but to eat their pack animals raw, for the barren landscape offered no brushwood to even kindle a fire. As a diversion, the guides pointed out the rock to which the Greek hero and demi-god Prometheus was believed to have been chained by Zeus.

Bessus, who had not been expecting the Macedonian army to travel through the Khawak Pass in winter, was terrified at his enemy's prowess. He lost his nerve and fled across the Oxus river into Sogdia, burning his boats behind him. Realizing Bessus would never stand and fight, his 8,000 Bactrian cavalry simply dispersed, leaving little opposition. Bactria's two major towns, Aornos (Tashkurgan) and Bactra, surrendered.

By filling their tents with straw to make them buoyant, the whole

Macedonian army managed to cross the fast-flowing Oxus river within five days. In Sogdia, Ptolemy captured the pretender Bessus, who had been abandoned by Spitamenes' men. When Alexander reached the regicide, who had been chained naked by the roadside, "he stopped his chariot and asked him why he had treated Darius, his king, kinsman, and benefactor so shamefully." Bessus answered that everyone close to Darius at that time had shared in the decision and their object was to "win Alexander's favor and so save their lives." The pretender was promptly flogged and sent back to Bactra for trial before a Persian court. After his nose and ears had first been cut off, he was publicly executed. Alexander was now free to march on to Samarkand (Maracanda), the royal city of Sogdia.

The Macedonian troops struggled over the Hindu Kush mountains (shown here) through snow drifts and biting winds, and suffering from chronic fatigue, snow blindness, and altitude sickness. As the army trekked upward, the king's unflagging determination was a tremendous motivating force, and often the only thing that kept his men on the move.

— 329–328BCE —

THE DESPOT OF SAMARKAND

In the summer of 329BCE, Alexander led his army through Sogdia to Samarkand (Maracanda). For the next 18 months, the Greeks used the town as a base from which to inflict a scorched-earth policy on the surrounding area. Local opposition centered on the Persian rebel Spitamenes, who, having initially cooperated with the invaders, now led a mass revolt against them, using guerilla tactics to great effect. Alexander found himself fighting a difficult and unexpected war. His response was at once desperate and ruthless—his soldiers massacred the adult male inhabitants of each defeated stronghold and enslaved the women and children.

Alexander marched on to the Jaxartes river (Tanais/Syr Darya), the north-eastern boundary of the Persian empire, where he pitched camp. After stiff resistance, the Macedonians eventually took six of the seven boundary forts that had been built by the Persians at strategic points as a defense against war-like local tribes. By the time his troops reached the largest Persian stronghold, Cyropolis, Alexander had already been wounded by an arrow through the leg. Although the Macedonians succeeded in taking the fort, and the Sogdians surrendered, Alexander was struck on the throat by a missile during the attack, causing him to temporarily lose his voice. A further blow to his head caused concussion and a temporary loss of vision.

Despite his wounds, Alexander set about planning another settlement—Alexandria-on-the-Tanais, also known as Alexandria Eschate, "the Furthest" (modern Khodjend). While they were reinforcing the site, the Macedonians had to fight off a hostile force of Scythians who gathered on the far bank of the Jaxartes. Alexander led the charge across the river. But in the intense heat, the king was driven to drink contaminated water and

THE MURDER OF CLEITUS

Alexander's attempts to follow Persian customs were constantly ridiculed by die-hard Macedonians such as Cleitus the Black. The king's patience was greatly tested by this, and matters came to a head at Samarkand in the fall of 328BCE. Plutarch describes a banquet during which Alexander and Cleitus became involved in a highly drunken exchange of insults. Cleitus—having reminded Alexander that he had saved his life at the Battle of the Granicus (see page 44)—taunted the king about his claims to divine paternity and his increasingly Persian ways, ending with the jibe "all your glory is due to your father." Unable to contain his anger, Alexander threw an apple at Cleitus, whose friends hurriedly bundled him out of the hall. Yet, fatally, Cleitus struggled free and blundered back in to deliver a new insult. Now beside himself with rage, Alexander seized a spear and ran Cleitus through, but was then instantly overcome with remorse and had to be restrained from taking his own life. After wallowing in self-loathing for several days, he was eventually comforted by his philosophers' assurances that fate had killed Cleitus and that, as king, everything Alexander did was lawful and just.

A 5th-century BCE silver Persian drinking vessel. By 328BCE, heavy drinking had become a common feature of the Macedonian court. One source says that Alexander "always had the tools for a drinking session with him."

was struck down with crippling dysentery. He fought on until he had to be carried back to his camp. This incident was followed by news that the small force sent to Samarkand to seek a diplomatic solution to Spitamenes' blockade of the fortress had been butchered by the rebel leader and his Scythian allies. Furious, Alexander set out at once with his best troops. On hearing of the king's approach, Spitamenes fled into the desert. The Macedonians' revenge was merciless—they systematically destroyed the area.

In the fall, Coenus and Artabazus were sent into Scythia in pursuit of Spitamenes while Alexander subdued a rebellion in Sogdia. He then returned to Bactra (Zariaspa), where he spent the winter of 329–328BCE.

ISKANDER THE ACCURSED

As Alexander advanced through the East, his reputation began to grow into legend. His very name came to evoke a mixture of awe and terror, and the people of each of the diverse regions of Asia Minor through which he passed created their own mythologies about him.

In one legend, Alexander's father was said to be none other than the Great King of Persia. Queen Olympias, it was claimed, had visited the court of Darius II and had captivated him with her beauty. Yet after only a single night, he had sent her back to Macedonia because she had bad breath, and so she began to chew the sweet herb chervil, known in Greece as "skandix." When her son was born she called him Sikander, which is also the Persian form of Alexander.

It was in Persia itself that the tales of Sikander Dhulkarnein, "the Two-Horned One," first emerged. For centuries, these stories were transmitted through the ever-changing oral tradition. They gradually developed into an epic worthy of Homer, and were later interwoven into the Islamic tradition. Although elements of truth are to be found in the tales of the two-horned Alexander—such as his defeat of the Persian king "Dara" and his respect for the tomb of King Cyrus—Sikander's destruction of the pagans in the name of Allah, his visits to China and the Arctic, and his voyages in a submarine are pure fantasy.

The versions of the Alexander legend that are recounted in Asia Minor today are complex and contradictory. In the 10th-century Persian epic the *Shahnama* (see page 81), which is still recited in modern Iran, Alexander is portrayed as the Shah of Shahs, the dying King Darius having bequeathed him his kingdom. Yet, in some religious folk plays, Alexander appears as one of history's greatest villains.

The Iranian Zoroastrians are the last surviving adherents of the ancient Persian religion followed by Darius and his forefathers. Alexander is still despised by the Zoroastrians as the evil, marauding invader who murdered their priests and destroyed their sacred book, the *Avesta*. They call him Iskander Gujaste—Alexander the Accursed.

A 16th-century Persian-school manuscript illustration depicting Iskander (top, center) and his army traveling through a desert. In Persian art, Alexander is often inaccurately portrayed as bearded and wielding a scimitar.

ROXANE THE FAIR

I t took the Macedonians another season to subdue Sogdia. Spitamenes was eventually executed by his own allies, following a defeat by Coenus. Alexander spent the winter of 328BCE in Nautaca, where he reviewed his system of governors, summoning those who had failed to present themselves at court. These included the Bactrian nobleman Oxyartes, whose wife and daughters were among the many local people who had taken refuge on the Sogdian Rock. The rock, garrisoned with 30,000 men, was believed to be impregnable.

Possessing the fine features shared by the Sogdian princess Roxane, and which so captivated Alexander, this sculpted head of a Bactrian noblewoman displays a wealth of jewelry and the fashionable hairstyle of the time.

Alexander advanced against the towering rock outcrop in early 327BCE. When he attempted to negotiate with the defenders, they simply laughed and told him to go and find soldiers with wings, otherwise he was wasting his time. Their ridicule only made Alexander more determined. He offered 12 talents to the first man to reach the top of the sheer-sided rock; three hundred men volunteered, and began their ascent up the steepest, least guarded part of the outcrop under cover of darkness. By dawn, 270 climbers had reached the summit. At their signal a delighted Alexander called on the Sogdians to surrender. Informing them that he had found "men with wings," he pointed to his soldiers who were lined up behind them. The Sogdians were so shocked they immediately surrendered themselves.

Among the Sogdians were Oxyartes' wife and daughters, one of whom was called Roxane (see page 96), meaning "little star."

According to Plutarch, Alexander fell in love with her "when he first saw her at the height of her youthful beauty dancing at a banquet."

Following his success at the Sogdian Rock, Alexander was encouraged to tackle a second rock fortress between the Oxus and Jaxartes rivers. Known as the Rock of Chorienes, or Rock of Sisimithres after the Paretiacae leader who sheltered there with his people, the rock was described by Arrian as 12,000 feet (3,650 meters) high, surrounded by a deep ravine, and sheer on every side. Alexander ordered his men to make ladders from local pines and bridge the ravine to allow the army to cross to the base of the rock. Having watched the Macedonians' approach with initial contempt and then growing alarm, Sisimithres sent a message to Oxyartes, who told him there was no point in opposing Alexander. Sisimithres surrendered the rock and was allowed to retain his position. In gratitude, he issued enough grain and dried meat to feed the Macedonian army for two months.

To the further delight of the local nobility, and amid lavish celebrations, Alexander married his Sogdian bride Roxane in the spring of 327BCE on the summit of the conquered Rock of Chorienes.

"Iskander and Rukshana" (Alexander and Roxane) are depicted in a scene from a Persian illuminated manuscript dated 1490CE.

INTIMATE COMPANIONS

A lexander had several close relationships that were of tremendous importance to him. He had a number of lovers, but also enjoyed strong platonic friendships and forged close ties with several maternal figures, including not only his mother Olympias, but also his childhood nurse Lanice and the queens Ada and Sisygambis, the mother of Darius.

Alexander seems to have determined at a young age that he would act more responsibly than Philip II, who caused his son and heir apparent much anguish by fathering several children with his numerous wives and mistresses. Perhaps as a result, for a long time Alexander showed little interest in forming sexual relationships. However, the adult Alexander, like his father, did have both male and female lovers. Bisexuality among men was common in Greek society, and the love felt by Alexander's great role model Achilles for his companion Patroclus reflected the king's feelings for his own lifelong partner Hephaestion. Although there is no direct evidence that Alexander and Hephaestion's relationship was sexual, the couple's visit to the Trojan graves of the two Homeric heroes served to publicly underline the nature and depth of their feelings for each other. Many members of the royal circle were jealous of their relationship, including Alexander's mother. In a letter to her, Hephaestion bluntly asks, "Why don't you stop quareling with me? Not that I care in any case. You know Alexander means more to me than anyone."

Despite his attachment to Hephaestion, Alexander was smitten by the beautiful Persian eunuch Bagoas, who had once been the attendant of Darius. Further evidence of the king's growing fondness for all things Persian, the young eunuch's grace and loyalty proved deeply attractive to

Although there are no firmly identified portraits of Hephaestion, this colossal bronze head attributed to Polycleitus may represent Alexander's beloved companion.

Alexander, and the two remained close for the rest of his life.

The king's attitude to women was unusual in the extreme for his day—no doubt influenced by his formidable mother, Alexander treated women with great respect. He regarded rape as a particularly terrible crime that should be severely punished, a philosophy he tried to impress upon his troops. Although some ancient sources refer to Alexander's relationships with various women (who, like his wives, were all Persian except for his Greek mistress Campaspe), according to Plutarch, Alexander "did not associate with any woman before his marriage [to Roxane] with the exception of Barsine." The daughter of the Persian nobleman Artabazus, and some 10 years Alexander's senior, Barsine became the king's lover after her Greek husband Memnon was killed at Issus. She is said to have borne Alexander's child, a boy named Heracles, who was later murdered.

In 327BCE, Alexander fell in love with the Sogdian princess Roxane (see page 94). Arrian reports that, although Roxane was a captive, the king "refused, despite his passion, to force her to his will and decided to marry her." As far as is possible to tell, the marriage was successful, both diplomatically and personally. The couple had a son, born posthumously, who was named after his father and succeeded him as Alexander IV (see page 155).

Alexander also later married two Persian princesses, Stateira and Parysatis (see pages 146–7). However, these seem to have been largely marriages of policy, meant to strengthen ties between Greeks and Persians.

THE KING'S FAVORITES

Plutarch writes that, like Olympias, Alexander's trusted general Craterus hated Hephaestion, but the two agreed to work together for the sake of their king, who needed them both:

"Alexander showed more affection for Hephaestion but more respect for Craterus. Alexander often said that while Hephaestion was a friend of Alexander's, Craterus was a friend of the king's. They were the two men he loved best in all the world."

—— 327BCE ——

THE PAGES' CONSPIRACY

As Alexander's empire continued to expand, it became more and more difficult to administer such culturally diverse areas. Their leader's appreciation of Persian customs was beginning to cause disaffection among the Macedonians, who now found they had to wait their turn for an audience with "their" king along with Persians and other foreigners. Alexander's request that all his subjects perform the act of *proskynesis* (the Persian ceremonial bow, see page 75) before a superior, was met with hostility from the Macedonians, who had only ever bowed down before divinity.

Despite growing dissent, Alexander was determined to create a fusion of customs acceptable to all, and he concocted a plan. Once Hephaestion had gained unanimous approval for *proskynesis* among leading Macedonians and Greeks, all were invited to a formal party at which they had agreed to share wine with the king and then perform a bow before rising to kiss him. Through the kiss—the traditional Persian mark of kinship—Alexander hoped to reassure his men that he was still one of them. All went smoothly until the philosopher Callisthenes, the court historian, stepped forward to kiss the king without first performing the required bow. Alexander seemed only to become aware of this when the Companion Demetrius pointed it out. When, as a result, Alexander refused to kiss Callisthenes, the philosopher remarked, "Well then, I must go back to my place the poorer for a kiss!"

Callisthenes, as his uncle Aristotle astutely observed, "may have possessed great eloquence, but lacked common sense." Greatly angered at such a public snub, Alexander began to question his historian's loyalties. Shortly afterward, there was a second plot against the king's life, led by a page called Hermolaus who bore a grudge against Alexander due to a personal slight. Together with several of the other pages, Hermolaus plotted to murder the king while he slept. However, on the night on which the pages planned to strike, Alexander—who had apparently been given warnings by a female Syrian visionary—stayed up drinking with his friends until dawn.

The following day, the disappointed conspirators began to gossip. Word of the failed plot soon reached Alexander and all those involved were promptly arrested. Ptolemy and Aristobulus both state that the conspirators then admitted that Callisthenes had "urged them to commit the crime." After the guilty pages' execution, Alexander wrote to Antipater, "The youths were stoned to death by the Macedonians, but as for the philosopher, I shall punish him myself, and I shall not forget those who sent him to me ... " Alexander's reference to Aristotle makes it clear that he suspected that even his former tutor had been involved in the plot. To publicly demonstrate his desire for justice, the king planned to send Callisthenes back to Greece to stand trial in the presence of Aristotle himself. However, before this could be arranged Callisthenes died in prison, "of excessive corpulence and the disease of lice," according to Plutarch.

As part of his attempt to fuse the diverse cultures of Greece and Persia, Alexander employed Persian bodyguards, such as the ones shown on this Persepolis relief, as well as Greeks. However, such obvious appreciation of Persian customs and skills was the cause of growing disaffection among his Macedonian followers.

CHAPTER FOUR

TO THE ENDLESS OCEAN

327–326BCE

This detail of an Attic Greek vase, dated ca. 480BCE, shows a warrior
wearing an Attic helmet and carrying a large, decorated shield.

THE LOST VALLEY OF THE GOD

In the late spring, Alexander resumed his advance east toward India, keen to extend his empire at least as far as the Indus river, the boundary set by Darius I more than 150 years before. Alexander's army recrossed the Hindu Kush in 10 days to return to Alexandria-in-Caucasus (near Begram). In early fall, the king led his troops down from the highlands and summoned all the Indian monarchs whose lands lay west of the Indus. Chief among these was King Omphis, also known by his dynastic title Taxiles, who ruled the territory between the Indus and Jhelum (Hydaspes) rivers.

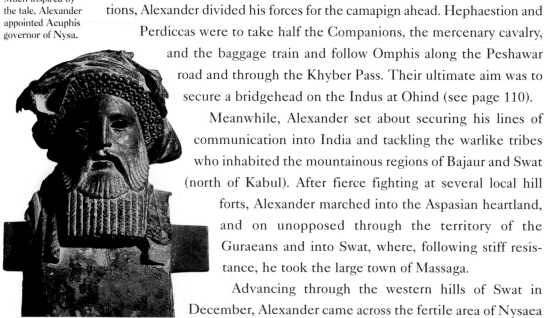

A Hellenistic bust of the Greek god Dionysus dating from the early–mid 3rd century BCE. As Alexander advanced into Swat, Acuphis of Nysa saved his city by claiming that it had been founded by Dionysus. Much inspired by the tale, Alexander appointed Acuphis governor of Nysa.

Omphis came before Alexander in October, bringing all kinds of exotic tribute, including 25 decorated elephants. Having established cordial relations, Alexander divided his forces for the camapign ahead. Hephaestion and Perdiccas were to take half the Companions, the mercenary cavalry, and the baggage train and follow Omphis along the Peshawar road and through the Khyber Pass. Their ultimate aim was to secure a bridgehead on the Indus at Ohind (see page 110).

Meanwhile, Alexander set about securing his lines of communication into India and tackling the warlike tribes who inhabited the mountainous regions of Bajaur and Swat (north of Kabul). After fierce fighting at several local hill forts, Alexander marched into the Aspasian heartland, and on unopposed through the territory of the Guraeans and into Swat, where, following stiff resistance, he took the large town of Massaga.

Advancing through the western hills of Swat in December, Alexander came across the fertile area of Nysaea

(Chitral). At the king's approach, a delegation from the local city, Nysa, came to ask that their town remain free and independent as a mark of respect for Dionysus. Their leader Acuphis related how the god had conquered India 6,042 years earlier, and, on his way home to Greece, "founded this city as a memorial of his long journey and his victory, leaving to inhabit it those of his men unfit for service." Acuphis recounted how the god had named Nysa in memory of his nurse, and had called the nearby Mount Merus ("the thigh") after his own fabled birth from the thigh of Zeus. In conclusion, Acuphis claimed that Nysa was the only place in India where Dionysus' sacred ivy plant grew.

An enthusiastic devotee of Dionysus, like his mother, Alexander found this story very much to his liking. He also recognized its propaganda value, for it gave him a chance to surpass the exploits of one of the great Greek gods. Suitably inspired, the king and his Companions set out to offer sacrifice at the site sacred to Dionysus on Mount Merus. Delighted to find the woodland overflowing with the laurels and ivies that reminded them of home, the Macedonians made wreaths of ivy, sang hymns of praise to the god, and, as Arrian writes, "lost their wits in true Bacchic frenzy."

Ruins in the fertile region of Taxila, close to modern Rawalpindi, Pakistan. The king of Taxila, Omphis, became Alexander's first Indian ally.

—————— 326BCE ——————

THE ROCK OF HERACLES

Alexander's objectives in early spring 326BCE were the strategic sites of Bazira (Birkot) and Ora (Ude-Gram) in the Choaspes valley. The inhabitants of Bazira refused to surrender, so the Macedonians built a stronghold outside the town and prevented the Bazirans gaining access to the surrounding countryside. Alexander had little trouble besieging Ora, and took the town on his first assault. When the Bazirans heard of their neighbors' demise, they abandoned their homes during the night, making for the safety of the Rock of Aornus (also known as Pir Sar, or "Rock of the Holy Man").

Ahead of the Macedonians' advance, thousands of Bazirans retreated to the strategic position of the rock. This natural formation rises 8,000 feet (2,440 meters) above the Indus river. The occupants of its flattened plateau must have felt reasonably secure, with a constant water supply from natural springs and plenty of arable land.

Alexander saw the rock's reputed impregnability as a challenge. He needed to win control of Aornus to subdue the area and secure his lines of communication, but he also yearned to surpass the deeds of the Greek demi-god Heracles, son of Zeus, who was said to have failed to take the rock as he wandered the earth performing his twelve great labors.

Alexander discovered from local intelligence that possibly the only way to attack Aornus was from the slightly higher, adjacent ridge of Una-Sar. Although the two peaks were not far apart, they were separated by the 800-foot (245-meter) deep Burimar Ravine—a formidable obstacle.

Local guides revealed that there was only one path to Una-Sar's summit, and this was so narrow that troops would be forced to pass along it in single file. Ptolemy was sent ahead with a hand-picked force of lightly-armed troops. On reaching the summit, Ptolemy sent smoke signals back to Alexander. The king set out to join him, but was thwarted when Indian defenders appeared and succeeded in keeping the two Macedonian groups apart. The stalemate was only broken when Alexander managed to get a message through to Ptolemy with orders to attack from the rear when a pre-arranged signal was heard. As Ptolemy began to attack the Indians from above, Alexander led the rest of the army up the thickly-wooded slopes and forced his way through to join his officer.

From the snowy peak of Una-Sar, the Macedonians were able to look down on Aornus. Yet, moving along the ridge, they saw that they had no choice but to cross the immense ravine in order to reach the enemy. A plan was put into action to bridge the chasm. Working in constant relays night and day for seven days, the troops pushed tons of earth into the ravine and slowly created a causeway using firs cut from the mountainside. Although the Baziran defenders showered the workers with arrows, spears, and rocks, Macedonian catapults, siege engines, and artillery pushed their way forward and began to answer the attacks in kind. Realizing their fate was sealed, the occupants of the Aornus plateau begged for a truce, while planning to escape during the night. On hearing of their intentions, Alexander rushed their position. Most of the Indians were killed where they stood; some flung themselves from the cliffs in desperation.

The first to set foot on the rock, Alexander took full possession of the site that had defied Heracles to become the greatest besieger in history. Yet the king still intended to press on ever further east, into regions where even the gods themselves had never ventured.

The Macedonians named the rock of Aornus "the Rock of Heracles." They believed that the Indian cattle they saw branded with the image of a club proved that the Greek demi-god, portrayed in this bust, had once visited India.

THE FACE OF A CONQUEROR

This highly idealized marble head of Alexander, based on the Greek original from Thasos, is a Roman copy that captures the king's trademark wide-eyed expression and curling, leonine hairstyle.

Alexander the Great was a skilled propagandist and was fully aware of the power of the image in a world in which few were literate. Throughout his reign, he maintained close control over his own official portraiture, be it sculpted, painted, or carved.

The king's characteristic features were brilliantly captured by his favorite sculptor Lysippus, who, moving away from the archaic modes of composition found in flat relief work, was one of the very first artists to create fully three-dimensional forms. Lysippus was revolutionary in his approach to his subjects. His vivid portrayal of Alexander's hero in his composition "Heracles Epitrapezius" proved inspirational, and the king awarded the sculptor exclusive rights to portray him in similarly heroic mode. The result was a series of portraits that was endlessly copied in the centuries following Alexander's untimely death. The Roman writer Plutarch later sang Lysippus' praises: "The best likeness of Alexander which has been preserved for us is to be found in the statues sculpted by Lysippus, the only artist whom Alexander considered worthy to represent him. Alexander possessed a number of individual features which many of Lysippus' followers later tried to reproduce, for example the poise of the neck which was tilted slightly to the left, or a certain melting look in his eyes, and the artist has exactly caught these peculiarities." The most famous of these later reproductions is the so-called "Azara Herm" (see opposite), a Roman bust the face of which is copied from a composition in bronze by Lysippus entitled "Alexander with a spear."

Lysippus represented Alexander as eternally youthful, and his work captures something of the conqueror's nervous energy and excitable, impetuous nature. The sculptor always portrayed him with his characteristic features framed by his long, tousled hair, which was often said to resemble a lion's mane. The king's large, intense eyes gaze characteristically upward, as if toward distant horizons (see box, page 108). His nose is straight, while his mouth neither smiles nor is sullen, remaining closed, presumably, to hide teeth that resembled "little pegs," according to a description in the "Romance of Alexander" tales (see page 165).

None of the figures sculpted by Lysippus tells us a great deal about Alexander's height. Although he is known to have been shorter than both Hephaestion and Darius III of Persia—who is said to have stood 6.5 feet (2 meters) tall (see page 41)—this does not necessarily mean that the Macedonian king was short. Indeed, there are no contemporary references to Alexander's height being in any way unusual, not even in the scathing condemnations of the Athenians.

As was the nature of all Greek sculpture at that time, statues of Alexander would have been painted. Reflecting the king's origins, his hair would have been painted a fair to light shade of brown, while his complexion was probably portrayed as somewhat ruddy or tanned (see page 108). The artist would also have given Alexander's eyes their highly unusual coloring, with one painted grey-blue and the other dark brown to black.

Lysippus' painted statues of Alexander are said to have been incredibly lifelike. The one set up at the temple of Delphi, for example, was so uncannily accurate that even several years after the king's death Antipater's treacherous son Cassander found it completely terrifying. According to Plutarch, when Cassander—who had had good reason to fear Alexander when he was alive—came face to face with the statue, "the mere sight struck him with horror, so that he shuddered

On the base of the Roman "Azara Herm," copied from a composition by Lysippus, the following verse is inscribed: "The image, gazing Zeusward, might almost be saying 'Earth is MY footstool! Zeus, you can keep Olympus!'"

GAZING AT THE GODS

Almost all of the statues of Alexander created by Lysippus and copied by later sculptors show the king's head bent slightly upward and to the left. While this could simply be a self-conscious affectation—as adopted by Alexander's successors—it is equally possible that the pose could be the result of a minor deformity of the neck or shoulders, perhaps connected to an early injury of some kind.

On these statues and busts, Alexander's large, intense eyes are depicted gazing up toward heaven. This feature probably alludes to the king's claim that he had divine ancestry, and was also much copied by his successors. Alexander's supposed eye color of blue–grey and brown–black might also be intended to suggest the combination of earthly rule and divine power; the heavenly blue and earthy brown are both encapsulated within a divinely-inspired human expression.

A Roman copy of an original Greek bust depicting Alexander gazing heavenward. Some scholars believe that this stylized representation of the king's tousled hair may allude to solar rays, and the portrait was perhaps meant to show Alexander as the sun god Helios.

and trembled in every limb, his head swam and he could scarcely regain control of himself."

Greek sculptors were not the only artists permitted to produce images of Alexander during his lifetime. Using skills perfected over millennia, Egyptian craftsmen combined traditional stylization with sculptural techniques learned from Greece in order to produce colossal figures of Alexander as Pharaoh, complete with the royal *nemes* headcloth and starched kilt (see page 51). Such images were repeated in relief scenes that were created to adorn the inner sanctuary of Luxor temple, in which Alexander is shown wearing the red and white Egyptian crowns.

Apart from Egyptian relief scenes, the only two-dimensional images officially sanctioned by Alexander were those carved on gemstones by his jeweler Pyrgoteles, and portraits by his favorite painter Apelles. The king held Apelles in such high regard that, when the painter was working on a portrait of the royal mistress Campaspe, Alexander gave her up when the artist and subject fell in love. Even so, Plutarch takes Apelles to task for his portrayal of Alexander's skin color (which the artist had perhaps portrayed, understandably, as somewhat weatherbeaten), bemoaning the fact

that, "when Apelles painted Alexander wielding a thunderbolt, he did not reproduce his coloring at all accurately. He made Alexander's complexion dark and swarthy, whereas we are told that he was fair-skinned, with a ruddy tinge that showed itself especially upon his face and chest."

However, the vast majority of Alexander's subjects would never have seen the official portraits created by his élite group of favored artists. For most of those who lived in the empire the king created, the only image they would ever see of him was that which appeared on his coinage (see page 68). Yet Alexander's face was rarely used on coins during his own lifetime (he preferred portraits of the gods), and only began to feature extensively on the coins minted after his death by his successors (see pages 154–7).

CROSSING THE INDUS

In the spring of 326BCE, Alexander and his vast army reached the banks of the formidable Indus. Arrian describes the wide, fast-flowing waterway as "bigger than any river in Europe, a mighty stream which imposes its name upon the country as it flows down to meet the sea." Alexander had already sent Hephaestion and Perdiccas ahead with half his forces to gather supplies and bridge the great river (see page 102). At a pre-arranged meeting point in the town of Ohind, some 16 miles (25 kilometers) above Attock, the Macedonian army was reunited and prepared to cross the Indus.

Although neither Ptolemy nor Aristobulus explain how this was done, Arrian states that the great depth of the Indus would have prevented Alexander's engineers (see box, opposite) from constructing a permanent bridge in the short time they had. Instead, he assumes that they must have created a temporary bridge by lashing together a large number of small boats in the same way Xerxes had once crossed the Dardanelles (Hellespont) and Darius the Great both the Bosphorus and Danube (Ister).

Once safely across the Indus, Alexander made his customary sacrifices to the gods. The lands of Taxila stretched before him as far as the Jhelum (Hydaspes) river. The kingdom's large and prosperous capital city Taxila (modern Bhir) lay at the junction of three major trade routes from Bactria, Kashmir, and the Ganges valley. Taxila was home to the region's ruler King Omphis (Ambhi), also known by his dynastic title of Taxiles.

Omphis had already pledged support for Alexander, and together with his officials and local dignitaries he was waiting to greet the Macedonians when they arrived in the city. With great ceremony, Omphis presented Alexander with 200 silver talents; 3,000 oxen; 10,000 sheep "for sacrificial

Boat bridges, similar to the one Alexander is thought to have built across the Indus river, can still be seen today. Across such a temporary structure the whole Macedonian army must have marched—some 64,000 infantry, 12,000 cavalry, and a baggage train including supplies, siege equipment, and hundreds of camp-followers.

purposes"; 30 elephants; and 700 Indian cavalry and 5,000 infantry. In return, Alexander offered his ally all the bordering territories he requested, together with a generous 1,000 talents in coin from his traveling treasury.

The kingdoms of the Punjab were deeply divided—Omphis was at war with his neighbor King Porus, whose kingdom lay to the east across the Jhelum. Alexander, who intended to capitalize on the kings' long-standing feud and their failure to produce united resistance, set up camp on the edge of Taxila and appointed the Macedonian Philip as district governor.

MILITARY ENGINEERING

Alexander's engineering corps played a key role in his campaigns, and their achievements remain unsurpassed. Whatever the terrain, from scorching desert to waterlogged marshland, they met every challenge they were set and overcame every difficulty they encountered.

Many of Alexander's victories were in large part due to the sheer inventiveness of his chief engineers Diades and Charias (both pupils of Polyidus of Thessaly). These engineers oversaw the production, by a team of highly skilled carpenters and metalworkers, of ever more effective equipment. Their battering rams, torsion catapults, ladders, platforms, and siege towers allowed the Macedonians to breach the most impregnable of strongholds. The engineering corp's bridge-building skills were equally outstanding. By 326BCE, when they were sent ahead of the rest of the army to bridge the Indus river, they had already successfully bridged the Euphrates, which was half a mile (750 meters) wide.

THE BATTLE OF THE ELEPHANTS

In May 326BCE Alexander and his ally Omphis (Taxiles) marched south to confront the forces of Porus. The Indian king, determined to prevent Alexander's advance into his territory, had made his intentions plain by massing his considerable force, including 200 war elephants, on the banks of the Jhelum (Hydaspes) river. Alexander knew that as soon as his cavalry horses sensed the elephants' presence they would panic, making it impossible to land them on the far side of the river in any sort of battle formation. He needed to find a way to transport the bulk of his army across the river without attracting the enemy's attention, allowing his troops the crucial element of surprise.

After the Battle of the Jhelum, Alexander commemorated his triumph over King Porus with this silver *decadrachm* (see also page 85). Alexander himself is depicted for the first time on a coin—he is shown astride Bucephalas, brandishing a *sarissa* against the Indian king, who is retreating on his elephant.

The Macedonians and their 5,000 Indian allies pitched camp beside the fast-flowing Jhelum near the modern town of Haranpur. Alexander resolved to find a secret crossing point to the north unbeknown to the enemy on the opposite bank. He feigned preparations as if he were about to cross close to the camp in order to test Porus' resolve. Macedonian troops repeatedly launched boats to simulate an invasion. Eventually, Porus ceased ordering his elephants forward to cover each feigned attack. The time had come to move—leaving Craterus behind to maintain the appearance of aggressive intent, Alexander led his forces away under cover of darkness.

Just before dawn, 18 miles (29 kilometers) north of their camp, the Macedonians crossed the river on boats, rafts, and straw-filled tent hides. As soon as they had landed under the wooded cover of the opposite bank Alexander set off to engage Porus. Suspecting that news of the enemy advance was another diversion, Porus sent his son with 2,000 cavalry to drive the Macedonians back into the river as they landed. But he was too late. The speed of Alexander's advance combined with his superior numbers won the day—400 of the Indians were killed, including the young prince.

Porus marched out to take on his fellow monarch. Knowing that the outcome of the battle would depend on how his infantry coped with the fearsome war elephants, Alexander planned to restrict the creatures' space as much as possible, forcing back the Indian cavalry. The Macedonian king launched the attack, leading the Companions and 1,000 mounted archers against the Indian cavalry. As Coenus attacked at the rear, the Indians were forced to fight on two fronts, and Porus' army was gradually surrounded. The Indians ran for the cover of the elephants, only to find them maddened by the Macedonian infantry's repeated attacks. In complete disarray, most of the Indians were slaughtered where they stood. Following the most appalling scenes of bloody carnage, Indian losses numbered some 20,000 infantry and 3,000 cavalry. Macedonian losses are said to have been as little as 80 infantry and 230 cavalry.

Porus, who had lost two more sons, bravely fought on until he was wounded in the shoulder, whereupon he turned to leave the field. Alexander sent a messenger to persuade Porus to surrender; the two kings finally came face to face in the midst of the battlefield. Full of admiration for the Indian ruler, the Macedonian asked Porus how he wished to be treated: "As a king," came the answer. "And what would you ask for yourself?" asked Alexander. "The words 'as a king' contain all I require," said Porus. This reply so impressed Alexander that he immediately restored Porus' sovereignty. In return, the warrior king remained loyal to Alexander until the end of his reign.

Having witnessed the ferocity of elephants in battle, and well aware of the fear they could instill in the enemy, Alexander very soon acquired some of his own. Here, the Macedonians' war elephants are depicted in a 15th-century French edition of Curtius' *Life of Alexander*.

LIFE ON THE MARCH

Most of the ordinary soldiers—Macedonians, Greeks, and foreign recruits alike—who followed Alexander across the known world encountered great extremes of fortune—they suffered terrible hardships, yet also enjoyed extraordinary success and riches. They campaigned deep into lands with which even their gods were unfamiliar. By the time they were sent home, many of the Macedonian veterans had served abroad for more than a decade. They had had to accept the recruitment of "barbarian" soldiers to their ranks, and had even witnessed their leader's partial adoption of Persian dress and customs.

Under Alexander's leadership his men never lost a battle, and their losses on the field were relatively few compared to those of their foes. The Macedonians' real enemies were the harsh conditions they endured en route. Thousands of Alexander's soldiers died of thirst crossing the burning deserts of North Africa and central Asia. Countless more perished in the freezing wastes of the Hindu Kush and Himalayas. A large number of Macedonian troops died from food poisoning, and even starvation when rations ran low. An invisible army of mysterious diseases and infections ravaged their numbers, and many men died from what would otherwise be non-fatal injuries when wounds festered in India's monsoon heat. Endless campaigning in such conditions inevitably took its toll on morale. Often the only thing that kept the men going was the sheer determination of their king, whose ability to motivate them, however terrible the circumstances, frequently bordered on the miraculous.

Yet, despite the hardship of life on the march, Alexander's soldiers experienced something few have ever known. Following an invincible king, who led them to victories they could have never imagined, they conquered

Perhaps left behind by one of Alexander's soldiers, this 4th-century BCE bronze Boetian helmet of the kind worn by members of the Macedonian Companion Cavalry was found in the Tigris river.

ALL THE KING'S MEN

A great deal of Alexander's success was due to his excellent relationship with his rank-and-file soldiers. Although various attempts on his life were made by disaffected members of the élite, the king retained the loyalty of the ordinary soldier to the end. Even when, on several occasions, he offered his men the chance to return home to Macedonia, many chose to stay and fight on, and he rewarded their loyalty with generous payouts.

The Macedonian troops regarded Alexander as one of them. He lived in their midst under canvas, sharing the same food, the same hardships, and the same challenges. Above all, he was always at their head, for Alexander led from the front—he was often the first across a river or over enemy lines, knowing his example would inspire his men with the confidence to succeed. He addressed his soldiers before every battle. After each encounter he visited the wounded, comparing battle scars and exchanging stories, listening to his men's experiences and allowing them to exaggerate their exploits.

A relief from a Nereid freize from Xanthos, dated 400BCE, depicts Greek soldiers marching shoulder to shoulder.

civilizations thousands of years older than their own, taking one opulent city after another to became wealthy beyond their wildest dreams. Alexander allowed them as much booty as they could carry (although looting was carefully regulated). Most of his soldiers also acquired foreign wives and children en route—the size of the baggage train and group of camp followers grew steadily until it rivaled that of the army. The soldiers who survived could confidently expect a comfortable retirement spent basking in the glory and material rewards of Alexander's campaigns.

—— 326BCE ——

THE DEATH OF BUCEPHALAS

Alexander's elation following his great victory on the banks of the Jhelum in May 326BCE was cut short by the death of his favorite horse, Bucephalas. Having accompanied his master to the ends of the known world, the legendary creature seems finally to have fallen victim to exhaustion and old age, although his demise may have been hastened by wounds inflicted on the battlefield. Alexander, it is said, "was plunged into grief at Bucephalas' death, feeling he had lost nothing less than a friend and a comrade."

This Achaemenid Persian horse's head, dating from the 5th–4th century BCE, is from the region of Takht-i-Kuwad, Tadjikistan.

Plutarch estimated that Bucephalas was around 30 years old when he died. Jet-black save for a distinctive white mark on his forehead, he had been named "oxhead" (Greek *bucephalus*) after the distinctive brand mark of his former owner, the Thessalian horse breeder Philoneicus. One of the defining moments of Alexander's life was the day when, as a boy, he alone had managed to tame the high-spirited stallion (see pages 18–19); Bucephalas had never tolerated any other master. Alexander rode to many great victories on his beloved steed, including those of the Granicus, Issus, Gaugamela, and the Jhelum. However, toward the end of Bucephalas' long life, Alexander had begun to use the horse increasingly sparingly in battle, keeping him in reserve until the final victory charge in which the two always shared, and otherwise only riding him during hunting trips.

Only once were horse and master separated. Around 331BCE, Bucephalas was stolen by Uxian horse thieves. Alexander's rage knew no bounds. He threatened to have every man, woman, and child in the country killed unless his horse was brought back. Bucephalas was immediately returned—evidence, as Arrian wrote, both of "the fear which

Alexander inspired and of his devotion to Bucephalas."

Alexander buried Bucephalas with every honor. The king then laid the foundations of two new cities by the Jhelum river: Nicaea after his victory over Porus, and Alexandria Bucephala in fond remembrance of a faithful companion. Although Alexandria-on-the-Tanais was the city referred to as Alexandria "the furthest," the most remote of Alexander's cities was the one built deep in the Indian Punjab in honor of its founder's legendary horse. Later tales claimed that Bucephalas, like his master, had had horns. Such stories may not have been completely unfounded—it is likely that golden horns were attached to Bucephalas as part of his decorative battle armor.

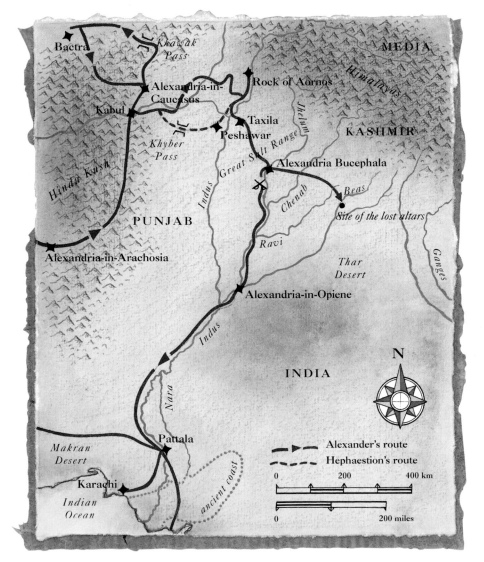

This map shows the site of Alexandria Bucephala, Alexander's journey from Alexandria-in-Arachosia to the Beas, and his route to the Indian Ocean.

—— 326BCE ——

A TIME OF HEAT AND RAIN

In late June, Alexander awarded his men a month's rest in Poros' fertile territory. Funeral rites were performed for those who had fallen in the Battle of the Jhelum, after which traditional games were held. Such a timely reaffirmation of a shared Greek heritage must have been in part designed to lift spirits severely dampened by the onset of the monsoon season. Nothing escaped the incessant downpour—the men's clothes became moldy and rotten, their armor rusted in a matter of hours, and it became only too clear that the lands ahead would be either flooded or knee-deep in mud.

A detail from a 6th-century BCE Greek black-figure krater. This ship is no doubt similar to some of the larger vessels the Macedonians incorporated into the mighty fleet that was to navigate the Jhelum and Indus rivers.

The inclement weather also brought with it the threat of bites from huge mosquitoes or the poisonous snakes that sought out dry areas inside the men's tents, clothing, and even cooking utensils. Although fatalities were kept to a minimum with the help of local snakecharmers, whose antidotes concocted from herbs and roots had been refined over centuries of use, the men were forced to sleep in makeshift hammocks above the ground.

While his men rested and sheltered from the rains, Alexander continued to make plans for the future. Summoning an Assembly of his Macedonians, he told them that India was now conquered, all its wealth was theirs, and all that remained was to advance to the furthest limit of India, where it was believed they would soon reach the waters of the Endless Ocean—the edge of their empire and of the known world. With the promise of support from the Assembly, Alexander decided he would reach his destination most easily and most rapidly by sailing down the

Jhelum river to the Indus and then into the Endless Ocean, "that he might look upon the end of the earth, the sea, when he had overrun all Asia," as Curtius later wrote. In order to achieve this, Alexander required a fleet large enough to carry his great army. A total of 1,800 vessels was needed, from 30-oared warships to troop carriers and cargo boats.

Vast quantities of timber had already been cut from the wooded foothills of the Himalaya mountains and floated down the Jhelum. (Alexander had given orders for firs and cedars to be felled well in advance to give the wood time to be seasoned and dried out.) Teams of local crafts-men and experienced shipwrights from the Mediterranean were now set to work to build the fleet. Once complete, this impressive navy would be manned by helmsmen and oarsmen from the sea-faring nations of Greece and its islands, Ionia, Phoenicia, Cyprus, and Caria, along with Egyptians used to navigating great rivers and local boatmen familiar with the hazards of their native waterways. Amazingly, the mammoth task of building the huge fleet was completed in just six months (see page 138).

The broad Indus river today. Moored along the bank are local craft similar to the ones Alexander commandeered to form a small part of his giant fleet.

OF BANYANS AND BRAHMINS

Long before his journey across the subcontinent, Alexander the Great had been fascinated by India. Since boyhood, the king had no doubt been familiar with the somewhat fanciful accounts of Herodotus, whose knowledge of India was based entirely on hearsay. Alexander's former tutor, Aristotle, who like Herodotus had never seen India, had described it as the furthest land mass east, beyond which lay only the Endless Ocean that encircled the world (see page 128).

During their time in India, in their attempts to understand and relate to this mysterious land, the Macedonians tended to equate major geographical features with those they already knew. Alexander referred to the Indus as the "upper Nile." For a while, he believed the Indus to be the source of that great Egyptian river, because it shared similar flora and fauna, including crocodiles. Alexander even planned to sail down the Indus and on to Egypt, although, as his admiral Nearchus writes, "not long afterward he discovered his mistake." However, by proving that the two great waterways were completely independent, the Macedonians dramatically changed the map of the ancient world, which hitherto had been based partly on supposition.

The Macedonian invaders also linked some Indian sites with their own deities and legends. They believed that the city of Nysa in the western Swat hills (see pages 102–103) had been founded by the Greek god Dionysus, and labeled the Rock of Aornus in the Choaspes valley (see pages 104–105) the "Rock of Heracles."

The historian Aristobulos of Phocis and Onesicritus of Cos (steersman of the fleet and a former student of the philosopher Diogenes) were among those who wrote commentaries on India during the Macedonian army's travels. Alexander and Hephaestion both sent letters describing the wonders of India back to Aristotle in Greece, while Nearchus compiled a detailed account of everything they encountered on their Indian journey—Arrian later used this work as the basis of his *Indica* (*History of India*).

Nearchus was able to report, "the Indians are slim. They are tall and

In contrast to Alexander's peaceful meeting with the Hindu philosophers the Greeks called "Gymnosophists" (see pages 122–3), portrayed in this 16th-century CE Indian miniature, the king's encounter with India's Brahmin priests was far from peaceful. By advocating a "holy war" against the invaders, the Brahmins incited widescale rebellion. At their instigation, all along his route down the Indus, Alexander was to meet some of the fiercest resistance he had ever faced.

much lighter in weight than other men ... they dye their beards, some of the very whitest of white, others dark blue, red, or purple, or even green. Their clothes are of linen ... they dress in a tunic down to the mid-calf and throw an outer mantle round their shoulders: another is wound round their head ... They wear shoes of white leather, elaborately decorated, the soles of which are thickened to make them seem tall. All except the very humblest carry parasols in summer." Alexander's admiral also wrote about Indian social customs, as did Onesicritus and Aristobulos. The Greeks seem to have found the Indians' treatment of women particularly curious, noting that

A 4th–5th-century BCE statuette of *devas* and *bodhisattvas* from Gandhara, the northwest frontier region of India, displaying the fusion between traditional Indian art and Greek classical forms—another legacy of Alexander's Indian campaign.

while an elephant was often given as a wealthy woman's dowry, "those who are too poor to give their daughters a dowry sell them in the market-place." Some such women were even awarded as prizes in boxing matches. Yet it was the barbaric practice of *suttee*, in which widows were burned alive on their husband's funeral pyre, that most shocked the Greeks. Alexander also strongly objected to the Indian practice of exposing their dead to be eaten by dogs and vultures instead of giving them a "proper burial."

Wherever he went, Alexander was in the habit of seeking out the local intelligentsia in an attempt to increase his understanding of cultures that were often very different to his own. In India, just as he had done in Egypt and Babylon, the king was keen to meet philosophers. During his two-month stay at Taxila (see page 110), he spent much of his time with teachers and religious figures. These included a group of local Hindu philosophers whom the Greeks dubbed "the Gymnosophists," or "Naked Philosophers," as they had renounced all worldly possessions, including clothing. The Gymnosophists chose to remain apart from the world around them, living outside the city. Alexander sent Onesicritus, a former student of the Cynic school of philosophy, to meet them. Dandamis, the leader and eldest of the 15 philosophers present, "commended Alexander for his love of wisdom even though he ruled such a vast empire—he was the only philosopher in arms he had ever seen. He went on to ask about Socrates, Pythagoras, and Diogenes, remarking that they seemed to be decent men, despite the fact that they paid too much attention to convention and not enough to nature."

One of the Gymnosophists, Sphines (whom the Greeks called Calanus), joined Alexander's entourage and accompanied the king on his return to the west. (The two men remained close friends until the

A LAND OF NATURAL WONDERS

The extraordinary fauna and flora they came across in India were a constant source of amazement to Alexander's followers, and his botanists excitedly recorded what they saw.

Crocodiles, scorpions, and enormous snakes alarmed the Macedonians. They were astonished by tigers so large they would even attack elephants—the mighty beasts of which the soldiers had had their first glimpse at the Battle of Gaugamela. The first time the troops heard monkeys' cries, they mistook them for the sounds of an unseen enemy army. Peacocks were another novelty —their beauty so impressed Alexander he forbade his men to hunt them.

Even Indian trees caused amazement: as well as great firs, Himalayan pines, and cedars up to 20 feet (7 meters) in circumference, there were also giant banyan trees "whose shoots spread out like a tent with many pillars, so wide 50 horsemen could shelter from the sun beneath it."

India's great variety of exotic plants must have been of particular interest to the botanist Theophrastus, who, like Alexander, had been a pupil of Aristotle. Although the small fruit of the banyan were found to be delicious, the Greeks' first encounter with the banana proved less successful. Described as "pods like a bean, ten inches long, and sweet as honey," this bizarre fruit gave the soldiers stomach-ache, and Alexander had to order them to leave it alone.

---

philosopher's death in Susa in 324BCE.) Alexander's encounter with the Gymnosophists—unlike that with the Brahmin priests (see caption, page 121)—was one of the highlights of his Indian expedition, and soon passed into the legends of both east and west. It was mentioned in the Alexander sagas and the Buddhist "Sayings of Milinda," and versions of the tale re-emerged in Renaissance Italy and even 17th-century England, where the Gymnosophists were regarded as Puritan role models.

The most tangible legacy of Alexander's time in India long remained the cities he built there (see pages 60–61). Towns such as Nicaea and Alexandria Bucephala on the Jhelum, Alexandria-in-Opiene at the confluence of the Indus and Acesines rivers, and Sogda and Pattala on the Indus were to outlive their famous founder by hundreds of years. Yet Alexander's true genius lay in his ability to combine Greek culture with that of the lands he conquered, skilfully blending them together to produce a hybrid acceptable to the majority of the population. As a result, archeologists are still discovering statues of Heracles, bronze heads of Dionysus, carvings of the Trojan Horse, and even figurines of Egyptian gods deep in the heart of India.

--- 326BCE ---

IN THE SHADOW OF THE HIMALAYA

In late July or early August, at the height of the monsoon season, Alexander mobilized his army. Accompanied by their Indian allies Porus and Omphis, whom Alexander had recently reconciled, the Macedonians marched eastward toward the foothills of Kashmir. News of Alexander's great victory at the Jhelum had gone before him—the neighboring Glausae tribe had already decided that resistance would prove futile, and Alexander handed more than 30 local settlements over to Porus. After a difficult crossing of the Chenab (Acesines) river, he led his troops on to the banks of the Ravi (Hydraotes).

Before crossing the Ravi, Alexander put down a rebellion led by his Indian ally's estranged nephew and namesake "Bad" Porus. This minor victory was followed by alarming news—the fiercely independent Cathaioi tribe, reported to be formidable opponents, were preparing to make a stand with the support of some of their neighbors at the town of Sangala (somewhere in the modern district of Amritsar, Pakistan).

After a rapid advance, the Macedonians reached the Cathaioi's stronghold to find it protected by three lines of fortifications encircling the slopes leading up to the town itself. The Indians refused to be drawn out of their defensive positions, so Alexander led an infantry assault which soon succeeded in overrunning the Cathaioi's first line of defense. After fierce hand-to-hand combat at the second defensive ring, the Indians retreated within their innermost walls. Alexander called a halt to the offensive as dusk fell. During the night, Cathaioi attempting to escape under cover of darkness were halted mid-flight. Around 500 Indians were killed; the rest retreated through the mud back into their stronghold.

As dawn broke, Alexander ordered his siege engines to be brought

forward. These would occupy the defenders' attention while his sappers undermined the brick-built fortifications. Scaling ladders were placed all around the walls of the stronghold. As the Macedonians scrambled to the top of the enemy walls, fierce fighting resulted in the slaughter of 17,000 Indians. A further 70,000 were taken prisoner. Arrian adds that, although Alexander lost fewer than 100 men, as many as 1,200 of his soldiers, including a large number of officers, were wounded.

After subjugating all those who had supported the Cathaioi, Alexander had Sangala razed to the ground. His message was a clear—he would tolerate no opposition on his way to the Endless Ocean.

OVERLEAF The snowy peaks of the Himalaya tower above the broad Indus river in northern Pakistan.

—————— 326BCE ——————

TO THE ENDS
OF THE EARTH

In the late summer of 326BCE, the Macedonians followed up the destruction of Sangala by pacifying the surrounding region and handing the conquered settlements over to Porus, who was to install his garrisons there. With northeastern India now secure, according to Arrian, Alexander pressed on toward the Beas (Hyphasis) river, "bent upon still further conquest. So long as a single hostile element remained, there could, he felt, be no end to the war." Alexander had been told that the lands across the Beas were rich and fertile. They were said to be inhabited by well-governed people who were fine soldiers and whose many war elephants were conspicuous for their size and courage. "Such stories could not but whet Alexander's appetite for yet another adventure," writes Arrian.

For Alexander—who had already surpassed the deeds of the gods Dionysus (see page 103) and Heracles (see page 105)—the certainty of lasting fame was not enough. It was not only his love of adventure that drove him on, but also his great thirst for knowledge, his constant desire to discover the unknown. And for this reason, the lure of the eastern waters of the Endless Ocean, the vast expanse of water that the Greeks believed formed the boundary of the world, was proving irresistible.

By now it was clear that the Endless Ocean was not where Aristotle had predicted it would be. Like so many Greek assumptions about the region's geography, the philosopher's statement that the Ocean could be seen from the heights of the Hindu Kush had proved to be incorrect. However, the Macedonians continued to believe that the Endless Ocean lay beyond India. Although his soldiers—from whom the king was careful to keep such details—had no idea how far away the eastern coast might

Dated ca. 300BCE, this terracotta matrix for a head of Alexander was made by a member of the circle of Lysippus, the king's favorite sculptor (see pages 106–109). Alexander was often portrayed gazing into the distance, as though dreaming of ever greater exploits.

be, Alexander himself must have been relatively well informed as to what lay ahead. Once in India, his ally Omphis would have been able to provide reasonably accurate geographical information. His capital Taxila was a thriving cosmopolitan urban center located on the great trade route to the east, and the town's distance from the shores of what is now known as the Bay of Bengal must have been common knowledge. Furthermore, the city was a great center of Hindu learning, and students from Taxila often traveled the length and breadth of the subcontinent to complete their studies. King Porus would also have been able to supply valuable information about the nature of the terrain and any opposition the Macedonians might expect. Armed with this knowledge, Alexander was determined to push on to the great Ganges river, some 200 miles (320 kilometers) to the east, conquer the kingdom of Magadha that lay beyond (see page 132), and march on to the very ends of the earth.

THE FINAL FRONTIER

As they approached the rain-swollen Beas river, Alexander and his troops halted near Lahore before the walls of the capital of the Indian king Sopeithes. The monarch himself—a tall, imposing figure, dressed in gold-and-purple robes of state—bravely came out to face the Macedonian army. Sopeithes signified his submission by handing his impressive jewel-encrusted scepter over to Alexander, who immediately reinstalled him as king. The Macedonians enjoyed several days of feasting and relaxation while their host entertained them with hunting displays by his fearsome dogs. Bred partly from tigers, the hounds so impressed Alexander that he was presented with one as a gift.

Alexander was now keen to press even further in his search for the eastern shores of the Endless Ocean (see pages 129–30). But in his fervor to reach his ultimate goal, he had uncharacteristically miscalculated the mood of his men, of whom Arrian notes, "The sight of their king undertaking an endless succession of dangerous and exhausting enterprises was beginning to depress them and their enthusiasm was ebbing."

For eight years the Macedonian soldiers had fought their way over difficult terrain in searing heat, freezing snow, and monsoon rains. Plutarch states that the Battle of the Jhelum, "had blunted their courage and made them determined not to advance any further into India." Soon rumors were circulating that, if they went on, they would have to cross an enormous river and face countless armies and their giant elephants. (There was some truth in this: the elephants in the region beyond the Beas were of a breed that was fiercer and larger than any the Macedonians had so far encountered). This was a prospect that filled the men with utter dread.

The rank-and-file soldiers who had, until now, followed Alexander without question, were desperate to leave the horrors of Indian campaigning behind and begin the long march home. Worn down by months of endless rain, alarmed by strange and to them barbaric customs, and shaken by the sheer ferocity of countless armies of opponents, the Macedonian troops had reached the limit of their tolerance. They were exhausted, their clothes were in rags, their equipment was rotten and rusty, and many of them were sick. In the foothills of Kashmir they mutinied, refusing to cross the Beas river.

Alexander took their disaffection seriously. He appeared before a meeting of his weary officers to give a typically rousing speech. Recalling shared hardships, past struggles, and their ultimate victories, the king urged the mutinying soldiers to go on. He promised that all of them could go home to Macedonia once they had reached the Endless Ocean's eastern waters.

A 14th-century Armenian copy of the 5th-century CE manuscript the "Romance of Alexander" portrays the king pleading with his mutinying officers on the banks of the Beas.

For the first and last time, Alexander failed to win over his officers—the men remained unmoved. It was left to the plain-speaking general Coenus to bravely speak out, pleading with Alexander to change his mind. Many of the officers wept as they listened. A stunned Alexander still hoped his men would reconsider, but when fresh appeals failed to sway them he sulked in his tent for two days. On day three he called for a sacrifice to test the omens for crossing the river and marching on. The conveniently adverse response as interpreted by the official military seer finally made the king relent and he gave the order to turn back. Alexander had reached the furthest extent of his astounding conquests—his empire stretched from the Balkans down to Nubia and across to the Punjab. The Beas river was to be its eastern frontier.

The Macedonian troops were overjoyed to be going home at last.

Many of them wept openly, and all their anger disappeared. Their leader's sole "defeat," they said, was "a victory of his kindness." Determined not to lose face, Alexander managed to turn a potential disaster into a triumph. With his usual flair for spectacle, he ordered magnificent equestrian and athletic games to be held in celebration of his momentous decision. He also honored 12 of his favored gods with great altars (see pages 136–7) to mark the limits of his empire.

However, in spite of such public displays of reconciliation, Alexander would never quite be able to forgive his men for their mutiny at the Beas. The king was only too aware that, had the army agreed to go on across the river, he could have added even more territory to his enormous empire with a minimum of effort from his men. Intelligence reports had informed Alexander that beyond the Ganges river—an easy march away—lay the kingdom of Magadha, which Porus told him was ruled by a weak, unpopular king. Indeed, only 10 years after the Macedonians erected their altars by the Beas, Magadha was conquered by the Indian king Chandragupta Maurya. The latter would later remark, according to Plutarch, "Alexander had been within a step of conquering the whole country, since the king who ruled it at that time was hated and despised because of his vicious character and lowly birth." To the east, Magadha stretched to the Bay of Bengal. The Macedonians had come within three months' march of the eastern edge of the known world. If only his men had agreed to follow his lead, Alexander knew that his greatest desire would have been fulfilled.

ALEXANDER ADDRESSES HIS OFFICERS

"... why do you hesitate to extend the power of Macedon—your power—to the Hyphasis [the Beas] and the tribes on the other side? Are you afraid that a few natives who may still be left will offer opposition? Come, come! These natives will either surrender without a blow or leave their country undefended for your taking ...

"... let me tell you that the area of country still ahead of us, from here to the Ganges and the Endless Ocean, is comparatively small ...

"... if we withdraw now there is a danger that the territory which we do not yet securely hold may be stirred to revolt by some nation we have not yet forced into submission. Should that happen, all that we have done and suffered will have proved fruitless ... Gentlemen of Macedon, and you, my friends and allies, this must not be. Stand firm; for well you know that hardship and danger are the price of glory, and that sweet is the savor of a life of courage and of deathless renown beyond the grave."

GENERAL COENUS APPEALS TO ALEXANDER

"... precisely in proportion to the number and magnitude of the achievements wrought by you, our leader, and by the men who marched from home under your command, I judge it best to set some limit to further enterprise ...

"... Every man of them longs to see his parents again, if they yet survive, or his wife, or his children; all are yearning for the familiar earth of home, hoping, pardonably enough, to live to revisit it, no longer in poverty and obscurity, but famous and enriched by the treasure you have enabled them to win. Do not try to lead men who are unwilling to follow you; if their heart is not in it, you will never find the old spirit or the old courage.

"... Sir, if there is one thing above all others a successful man should know, it is when to stop. Assuredly for a commander like yourself, with an army like ours, there is nothing to fear from any enemy; but luck, remember, is an unpredictable thing, and against what it may bring no man has any defense."

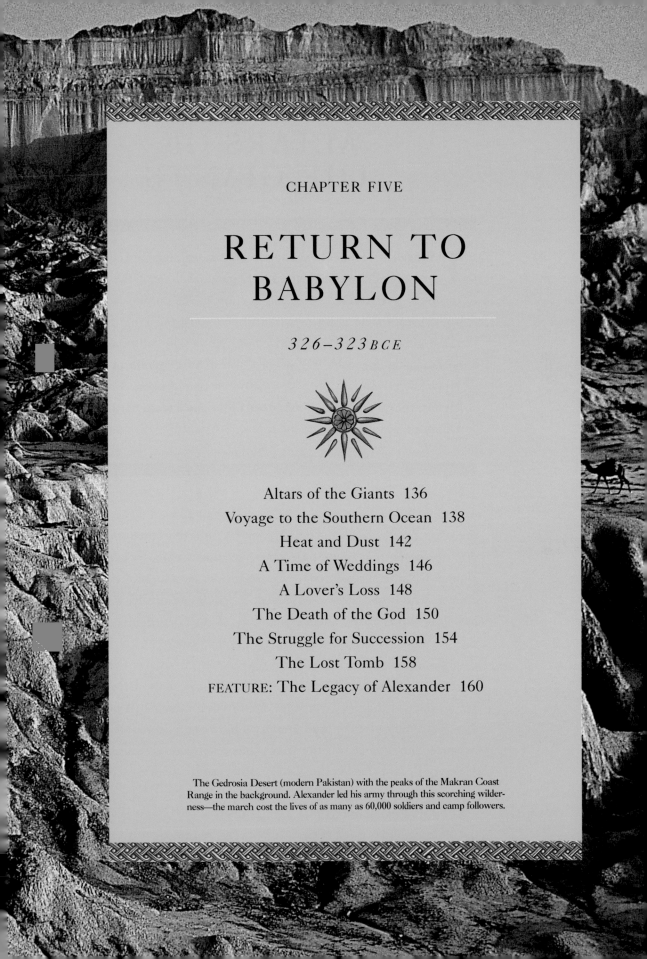

CHAPTER FIVE

RETURN TO BABYLON

326–323 BCE

The Gedrosia Desert (modern Pakistan) with the peaks of the Makran Coast Range in the background. Alexander led his army through this scorching wilderness—the march cost the lives of as many as 60,000 soldiers and camp followers.

—————————— 326BCE ——————————

ALTARS OF
THE GIANTS

In the fall of 326BCE Alexander divided his soldiers into companies and ordered the construction of 12 gigantic altars on the banks of the Beas river to mark the eastern limit of his empire (see pages 132–5). In a style befitting a son of the gods, the king dedicated these great altars to the deities whose protection had brought him so far, including Athena Pronoia ("foresight"), Apollo of Delphi, Heracles, Olympian Zeus, the Cabiri of Samothrace, Amun, and Helios, the sun. Although the other four names were not recorded, Dionysus was no doubt among them.

According to Diodorus, each altar stood 75 feet (23 meters) high. As tall as the loftiest siege tower, and designed to take offerings up to the very gods themselves, these mammoth structures would have been visible for miles around. Chandragupta Maurya (see page 132), founder of the first Indian empire, who is said to have glimpsed Alexander as a child, is reported to have worshiped at the altars in memory of the Macedonian king. That they survived for at least four centuries is clear from Plutarch's statement that, even in his time, the kings of that region "whenever they cross the river honor the altars and offer sacrifice on them in the Greek fashion." Yet no trace of the twelve altars has ever been found. It is possible that they were built of mere mudbrick, and have not survived. Alternatively, because the course of the Beas has changed considerably since Alexander's day, the river may have obliterated all trace of the altars or have simply hidden the site of their original location.

Philostratus mentions that a brass obelisk or column inscribed with the simple words "Alexander stopped here" was also erected at the site. If such an inscription existed, like the altars, it has never been found.

Several sources state that Alexander also "devised further ruses and deceptions to impress the inhabitants of the region" and discourage rebellion. It is said that the king ordered his men to construct a camp three times larger than normal. Its huts were equiped with extravagantly sized beds 8 feet (2.5 meters) long, with the stalls for horses built on a similarly massive scale. The aim of this strange enterprise, it is claimed, was to create the impression that the Macedonians were a race of giants, although, like the nearby altars, the camp of the giants has never been located.

With all completed to his satisfaction, Alexander consigned the hard-won territory west of the Beas to his ally King Porus. Yet, even as Alexander gave the order for the army to begin the long march that would ultimately take them home, their problems were far from over.

A 1st-century CE Roman stucco relief depicts Alexander enthroned between the Greek gods Poseidon and Heracles. To the latter was dedicated one of the 12 lost altars of the Beas.

326BCE

VOYAGE TO THE SOUTHERN OCEAN

A painted plaster model of a 4th-century BCE warship, its helmsman at the stern and the round shields of the soldiers within stacked along the sides as a defensive measure.

Alexander announced the resumption of his plans to "conquer all of southern India," and set off at the head of a huge column of 120,000 fighting men. Retracing their steps from the Beas river, the army marched back across the Ravi and Chenab rivers to Nicaea and Alexandria Bucephala, settlements Alexander had founded earlier that year. Despite heavy flooding, his carpenters and shipwrights were still hard at work on the river banks (modern Jalalpur), just as Alexander had left them earlier in the summer, building a fleet of ships that would sail on to the Southern (Indian) Ocean.

At around this time, Coenus (see page 131) became seriously ill, possibly as a result of the relentless rains and hot conditions. His death soon after was a great blow to the king, for Coenus had been a capable general and trusted friend. Alexander gave him a splendid funeral. He then organized a great meeting of his Companions and envoys from all over India, at which he proclaimed his faithful ally Porus king of all the territory from Taxila to the Beas.

As the fleet neared completion, Alexander began to re-organize his army in preparation for the difficult expedition that lay ahead. He split the Macedonian forces into three divisions. The king himself would travel by river, accompanied by a total of around 8,000 men. He placed Craterus on the right bank of the Jhelum, with part of the infantry and cavalry. The left bank was put under the control of Hephaestion, who was to command the main body of the army, together with 200 war elephants. As a final safeguard, the Macedonian satrap Philip would follow behind three days later in order to deal with any rebels who had avoided or escaped the main

army. It would be crucial to counteract any hint of subversion if vital lines of communication were to be secured in order to supply the fleet. Alexander then gave his land forces the order "to march with all speed to the palace of King Sopeithes," an unknown location somewhere near Lahore where the army had enjoyed royal hospitality only a few months earlier.

By the beginning of November 326BCE, the great fleet was ready to start its journey down the Jhelum river to the Indus and on to the Ocean. When Alexander finally gave the order for embarkation, almost 2,000 naval craft were assembled on the river. Most impressive of all were the 30-oared galleys (designed to Alexander's own specifications), of which there were 80, together with numerous supply vessels, smaller boats, and barges to transport the horses. The king appointed his boyhood friend Nearchus the Cretan as Admiral of the Fleet with Onesiscritus as his second-in-command and helmsman of Alexander's own ship. The vessels were manned by Phoenicians, Cypriots, Carians, and Egyptians, together with Indians who would help them to navigate the route.

As dawn broke on that early November morning, the king stood at the

In order to create his 2,000-strong fleet, Alexander would have supplemented his specifically designed war galleys by commandeering many of the existing local craft—similar to these modern boats at Kotri on the Indus—to act as supply vessels.

prow of his ship, held out a golden bowl, and poured generous libations into the fast-flowing waters of the Jhelum, asking the river for safe passage. He also invoked the waters of the Chenab and Indus, which they would encounter on their long journey down through the unknown lands of southern India, and offered sacrifices to the gods. Alexander then bade Porus a final farewell, and ordered the trumpets to sound as the signal for the fleet to cast off their moorings. The ships' purple-dyed sails were unfurled and caught the breeze, and the coxswains began to beat out the steady strokes for the oarsmen to follow. As the fleet moved off slowly down the river in strict formation, the local people came out of their homes to watch the spectacle, singing and dancing all along the steep banks (see box, opposite).

After three days, the fleet caught up with the land forces at a pre-arranged rendezvous close to the palace of King Sopeithes. Here they waited for two days to allow Philip's forces to catch up. Alexander then sent Philip on to the Chenab with orders to proceed along its banks and cover Hephaestion's left flank. Hephaestion and Craterus were ordered ahead "with careful instructions of the route they were to follow." Alexander himself resumed his progress down the Jhelum, which Arrian notes was wide enough for 40 war galleys to sail side by side.

The early stages of the epic voyage were uneventful. The tribes the Macedonians encountered were mainly peaceful, submitting at Alexander's impressive water-borne approach. Yet disturbing reports began to filter through that the Malli (Mahlavas) and Oxydracae (Kshudraka) tribes had joined forces to resist the Macedonians. At

This detail on an Attic black-figure vessel shows a multi-oared warship of the type Alexander's army used to sail down the rivers of India.

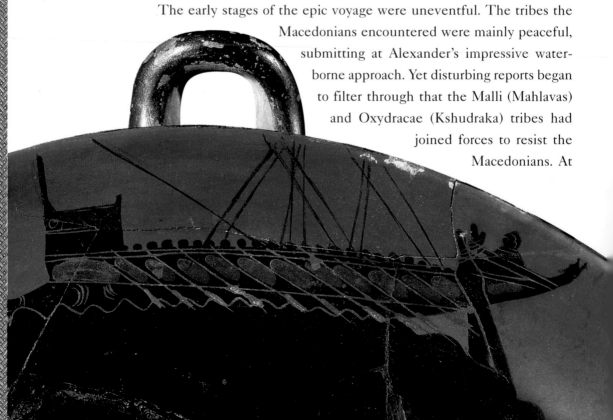

THE LARGEST FLEET EVER SEEN IN INDIAN WATERS

The sight of Alexander's ships sailing down Indian rivers made such an impression on eyewitnesses that even 400 years later, Arrian was able to compose a vivid account of it:

"One may imagine the noise of this great fleet getting away under oars all together: it was like nothing ever heard before ... The natives had never before seen horses on board ship, and the sight of them crowding the barges filled them with such amazement that all who witnessed the departure of the fleet followed it along the banks for miles, and other friendly tribesmen who were near enough to hear the cries of the rowers and the dash and clatter of the oars came running to the river bank and joined in the procession, singing their native songs."

this news, Alexander pressed on at optimum speed, eager to pre-empt the enemies' preparations and engage them. However, the fleet was now approaching the dangerous confluence of the Jhelum and Chenab rivers.

When they heard the mighty roar of the rapids ahead, the fleets' coxwains were struck dumb with shock. As Arrian writes, the helmsmen had to take control, "shouting out orders to the rowers to put their backs into it and drive through the narrows at full speed in the hope that this would prevent them from being spun round by the swirling eddies." Although the barges and smaller craft managed to get through largely unscathed, the larger galleys were less fortunate. Many of their oars snapped off and two of them collided in the foaming waters with the loss of many lives. When finally the river broadened out, the current eased sufficiently for the boats to moor so that the sailors could fish out survivors.

While essential repairs were underway, Alexander mounted a brief campaign against local tribes who he suspected might be tempted to collaborate with the Malli against him. Once his flank was secured, the king rejoined the fleet on the borders of enemy territory in preparation for the inevitable conflict with the fiercest of all the Indian warrior tribes.

— 326–325BCE —

HEAT AND DUST

In December 326BCE, Alexander was joined on the banks of the Indus river by Hephaestion, Craterus, and Philip on the borders of the territory of the Malli, the Indian tribe that was preparing rebellion. Alexander took a corps of soldiers to lead a dawn attack on the unsuspecting Mallians, whose walled town was soon taken. However, the few Mallians who managed to escape across the Ravi (Hydraotes) river eventually joined up with their allies to form a force of some 50,000, who sought refuge from Alexander's cavalry and infantry in the great fortress of Multan.

At dawn the Macedonians launched an attack against Multan's fortified defenses. Impatient, Alexander snatched one of the few available ladders and scrambled up onto the citadel's ramparts, followed by three of his men. But as the rest of the Macedonians tried to follow, their ladders shattered, leaving the four men isolated. The king—a clear target in his resplendent armor—and his three companions leapt down into the Indian fort, and were rapidly encircled. Alexander was critically wounded by an arrow which penetrated his corselet. Meanwhile the rest of the army were desperately trying to scale the walls. To their horror, those who managed to get over the top were met with the sight of their king lying wounded on the ground. Once the fortress gate was smashed, the whole army poured in; in their rage the Macedonians massacred all the defenders.

Alexander was carried away close to death. His wound was leaking blood and air, indicating that the arrow had pierced his lung. Arrian states that although some sources say the arrow was cut out by a doctor, others believe that Perdiccas cut it out with his sword at Alexander's request.

Believing their king to have died from his injuries, the troops back at the base camp were plunged into despair. Alexander, realizing that he must appear before them, demanded to be taken by ship to the camp. On arrival, he raised his hand in greeting and a great wave of relief swept through the ranks. When offered a stretcher to leave the ship, Alexander called instead for a horse, which he managed to ride to his tent amid deafening applause and cries of joy. Although the injured king was rebuked by Craterus and Ptolemy for risking his life in such a reckless way, his bravado had not been in vain—the Mallians and their allies surrendered.

After an all-too brief period of convalescence, Alexander continued downstream into the opulent kingdom of Musicanus. The latter initially submitted, but rebelled as soon as the invaders had moved on. Musicanus was eventually captured and hanged for his duplicity, along with the Brahmins who had incited his revolt. The ruler of Pattala (modern Hyderabad), wisely surrendered to the Macedonians. Impressed with Pattala's strategic location, which was then at the apex of the Indus delta, the king ordered Hephaestion to build dockyards, transforming the town into a major port. Alexander then set off down the western arm of the river to explore the Indus delta. He sailed out to sea to sacrifice bulls to Poseidon and pour libations

This map shows the routes that Alexander, Craterus, and Nearchus took from the Indus Delta back to Babylon. The troops and camp followers led by Alexander suffered terrible losses in the scorching Makran Desert.

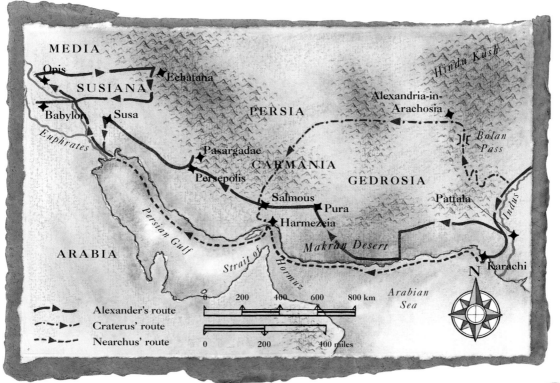

into the waters to ensure safe passage for the fleet before returning to Pattala to finalize arrangements for the long journey back to Babylon.

Alexander left Nearchus and the fleet to await the favorable winds of late September, and sent Craterus—with three phalanx brigades and thousands of demobbed veterans—from the Indus valley over the Bolan Pass into Iran. The king then mobilized the rest of his troops and the non-combatants in late August 325BCE. Instead of taking the relatively easy inland route west, they marched along the coast in order to leave supplies and dig a series of wells to provide the fleet with food and water as they followed on. In October, Alexander led his army toward Gedrosia and the Makran Desert. However, the shoreline, inhabited only by the primitive Ichthyophagi (Fish-eaters), provided little by way of supplies, and soon the Macedonians were forced to turn inland—leaving the fleet to fend for itself—into inhospitable conditions where the army marched by night to escape the searing heat. Wagons were unable to cross the sand dunes and quicksand and had to be left behind. Water and food began to run short; supplies that had been due to arrive by convoy never materialized, for Philip, the Macedonian satrap responsible for them, had been murdered. Baggage animals killed by exhaustion were eaten by the troops. Sunstroke, thirst, or exhaustion claimed many lives; those who fell by the wayside were left to die. One evening, when they were encamped by a small stream bed, a flash flood cost the lives of many of the camp followers. Soon afterward, all recognizable landmarks were obliterated by the waters and strong desert winds. The army was lost in a featureless desert until the king and a small band of soldiers found their way to the coast, where they discovered fresh-water springs.

Alexander shared his men's lot—when they had no horses he dismounted, when they had no food he refused to eat. When some of them had managed to find a

Gedrosia and the Makran Desert, shown here, were rich in exotic plants such as spikenard, which released its sweet fragrance as it was trampled by Alexander's soldiers. Little did they realize they were about to enter a blazing, waterless wilderness from which many would never emerge.

MEDICAL CARE

Doctors were valued members of Alexander's campaign personnel. As well as Greek-trained physicians, such as Philip and Glaucias, the Macedonians employed doctors schooled in the far older and equally sophisticated medical traditions of Egypt, Persia, and India.

Plutarch mentions that Alexander—having gained a great deal of medical knowledge from Aristotle's teaching—regularly enquired after his men's health and gave advice about the most effective treatments, even advising the doctors on the use of drugs such as hellebore. Depending on the region through which the army was passing, treatments made up from local herbs and roots and refined over long centuries of use were administered. Local knowledge was thus combined with standard Greek medicines and practices to treat disease and wounds alike.

A detail from a 5th-century BCE red-figure krater shows a Greek physician bleeding a soldier.

trickle of water in a small gully, they scooped it up in a helmet and took it back to Alexander, who must have been suffering terribly from the pain of his unhealed wound. He thanked them, and then, in full view of his troops, poured the water on the ground. "So extraordinary was the effect that the water wasted by Alexander was as good as a drink for every man in the army," says Arrian. Sixty days after entering the Makran Desert, the survivors arrived in the capital of Gedrosia in the district of Pura. The journey had been the worst disaster of Alexander's entire campaign—the army had lost thousands of men, women, and children.

Rejoined by Craterus in the Carmanian capital Salmous (Gulshkird), Alexander was becoming anxious about the fate of the fleet. In fact, the sailors had survived the ordeal of the journey by sea relatively unscathed, and eventually landed at Harmezeia (Hormuz). They had an emotional reunion with the king in late December 325BCE amid great celebrations.

324BCE

A TIME OF WEDDINGS

After his reunion with Nearchus at the end of 325BCE, Alexander sent the fleet on to the mouth of the Tigris, while Hephaestion took the greater part of the army westward along the coast into Persia. The king led the remaining troops to Pasargadae, where he ordered the repair of the tomb of Cyrus the Great (died 529BCE), founder of the Persian empire. In late February, Alexander and his men arrived in Susa, where the king's attempts to forge ever closer cultural links culminated in the ultimate public demonstration of unity—an extraordinary series of marriage ceremonies.

News that Cyrus the Great's tomb had been desecrated angered Alexander, who was keen to be seen as the true inheritor of Cyrus' throne. As he had done just five years earlier, the king once again ordered that the tomb, shown here, be completely restored.

These were marriages of policy. Alexander himself led the way by wedding Darius' eldest daughter Barsine, who was renamed Stateira after the mother she resembled. According to Aristobulos, the king also married a second Persian princess, Parysatis, the younger daughter of Artaxerxes III. In a ceremony watched by 9,000 guests, 92 Companions also took Persian brides and became relatives not only of Persians, but of each other. Hephaestion married Darius' second daughter Drypetis, because Alexander wanted the children of his closest friend to be his own nephews and nieces. Craterus married Darius' niece. Ptolemy was given Artabazus' daughter, Nearchus wed one of Artabazus' granddaughters, and Seleucus (see page 157) married a daughter of Spitamenes.

Alexander provided each bride's dowry, and a gave a wedding gift to each of the 10,000 or so Macedonian soldiers who had already taken Persian wives. To the further astonishment of the troops, he also announced that he would pay off all his men's debts—he spent 20,000 talents honoring his word. This is likely to have been an attempt by the king to gain his men's acceptance for such major cross-cultural innovations, as their patience with his policy of "Orientalization" was soon to be tested by the arrival in Susa of the 30,000 Persian youths Alexander had placed in training three years before. The new soldiers, writes Arrian, were "all wearing Macedonian battle-dress and trained on Macedonian lines." Although Alexander was clearly delighted with their progress, his Macedonian troops were not at all impressed, and felt they were being supplanted in the king's favor.

Alexander left Susa to sail down the Eulaeus river to the Persian Gulf, again exploring the potential for increasing trade links in the region. During his journey, he founded a new Alexandria (later called Charax) between the mouths of the Eulaeus and the Tigris rivers. Having left orders for Hephaestion to lead the main army overland to the Tigris, where Alexander would join forces with him as he returned north, the king sailed up the Tigris to Opis.

In Opis, the time came to send home—with generous payouts—those no longer fit for service. However, the Macedonian veterans, already furious about the new Persian recruits, whom they nicknamed the "ballet-soldiers," protested that Alexander "had first worn them down with every kind of active service, and now was turning them away in disgrace." Alexander flew into a rage, listing everything that he and his father Philip had done for them. He then withdrew completely from his countrymen, surrounding himself exclusively with Persian staff. This brought the Macedonians to their senses—they remained for two days and nights outside the palace, refusing to leave until, on the third day, the king forgave them. Following a great banquet, the placated veterans were sent home to Macedonia escorted by Craterus. The latter was to replace the ageing regent Antipater, who was to be summoned to bring fresh troops to Persia. Craterus' absence meant Hephaestion was now fully second-in-command. However, he would not live long to enjoy his new status.

The paintings on this Greek red-figure vase, dated ca. 450BCE, depict elaborate wedding preparations. Alexander's royal chamberlain Chares reports that the wedding ceremonies performed at Susa, during which Macedonian officers were married to Persian noblewomen, followed Persian, rather than Greek, custom.

324BCE

A LOVER'S LOSS

To escape the heat, Alexander and his army spent the summer and fall resting at Ecbatana (modern Hamadan). The king, his courtiers, and his first wife Roxane attended a series of plays—including comedies, which Alexander loved—put on by a group of traveling Greek performers. During these festivities, Alexander's closest friend Hephaestion developed a high fever, apparently brought on by excessive drinking. A week later the patient was showing signs of recovery, and the king left his side to spend a day at the stadium. While he was gone, Hephaestion suffered a fatal relapse.

A messenger was sent to Alexander, who came hurrying back, but arrived too late. Distraught, the king flung himself across Hephaestion's body, where he lay for the rest of the day in tears—in the evening he had to be dragged away by his Companions. For two more days, paralyzed by grief, Alexander refused to eat or drink. Emulating Achilles at the death of his lover and friend Patroclus, the king then sheared off his hair, and ordered that the manes and tails of all the horses and mules also be cut. It is said that he also had Hephaestion's doctor Glaucus either hanged or crucified for prescribing ineffective medicine, and ordered that the Ecbatana temple of the god of healing, Asclepius, be razed to the ground. "Asclepius," Alexander later remarked bitterly, "has not treated me kindly, for he did not save the friend I valued as my own life."

A state of general mourning was declared throughout the East. In all the temples of the empire the sacred fires were extinguished. Alexander ordered sacrifices to be made to Hephaestion and even sent envoys to Siwa to ask the Oracle of Amun (Libyan Ammon, see page 56) whether his friend could be elevated to the rank of a god. This request was refused,

This warrior from the 4th-century BCE "Alexander Sarcophagus" in Istanbul is believed to depict Hephaestion, the lifelong friend and lover of Alexander the Great.

but Amun's priests proclaimed that the deceased could be worshiped as a hero. A great stone lion was erected at Ecbatana as a memorial to Hephaestion, although the most extravagant monuments were to be set up "regardless of expense" at Alexandria in Egypt. Hephaestion's embalmed body was sent to Babylon, where Alexander planned to hold a spectacular funeral ceremony (see page 151). Alexander's distress was "long drawn out." In the winter, he sought to numb his grief through action, undertaking a 40-day campaign against the Cossaeans. He also appears to have sought comfort elsewhere—before the end of the year Roxane announced that she was pregnant with Alexander's heir.

—————— *323BCE* ——————

THE DEATH
OF THE GOD

As Alexander approached Babylon in April 323BCE, he was met by the priests of Bel (Marduk), who begged him not to enter the city, saying the oracles were strongly against it. Unwilling to delay his arrival, the king decided to enter Babylon from the east, which, according to the priests, would afford him some protection. Yet marshland made this an impossible route for the army, and Alexander was forced to take the West Gate into the city. He also chose to ignore warnings from Apollodorus, whose brother, a seer, had found grave omens concerning the king in his reading of the entrails of sacrificial animals.

While he was in Babylon, Alexander received delegations from across his empire and beyond. Many rulers of western kingdoms, mindful that the conqueror of the east was now looking westward in his endless quest for new territories, had wisely decided to demonstrate their allegiance. Of these delegations Arrian writes, "some of them even appealed to Alexander to arbitrate in their domestic quarrels, with the result that both he and his friends felt that he was indeed master of the world."

Although he was still deeply affected by the loss of Hephaestion, from his base in the great palace of Nebuchadnezzar Alexander nevertheless immersed himself in a range of ambitious projects. Chief among these was a campaign against Arabia, for the king was well aware that he had received no acknowledgment from the country which had in the past been a useful ally of the Persian rulers. Arrian states that Alexander planned to settle the coast of the Persian Gulf, "for he fancied it might become as prosperous as Phoenicia." If the king could establish a permanent sea route to Egypt, and utilize the pharaonic canal linking the Red Sea to the Nile river, he could exploit Arabia's enormous potential for

international trade. Alexander's shipwrights
were busy preparing a huge naval force that
was due to set sail on 5 June. Nearchus had
already brought the exisiting fleet to
Babylon, having sailed up the Euphrates from
the Persian Gulf, and here they were met by
another 50 or so Phoenician vessels, which
had arrived in sections overland.

    Once his plans for the Arabian
campaign were well underway,
Alexander was finally able to perform Hephaestion's funeral rites.
After months of careful preparation,
Hephaestion's embalmed body now
lay atop a spectacular wooden pyre in the
form of a 200-foot (60-meter) high ziggurat.
Each stepped level was gilded and painted,
and carved with hundreds of ornate figures
of soldiers, eagles, serpents, bulls, and lions
interspersed with Macedonian and Persian
weaponry. Once the flames were lit, the fur-
nace-like heat and sheer spectacle must
have amazed all who saw it.

    Having thus paid hommage to his
beloved Hephaestion, Alexander undertook a
brief tour of the local waterways and canals. He
wanted to inspect Babylon's complex irrigation
system, and also to visit the tombs of the Assyrian
monarchs. As the king sailed through the royal necropolis,
a gust of wind blew off his broad-brimmed sun hat with its
royal diadem. The sailor who retrieved it placed the diadem on his own
head to keep it from the murky waters, not realizing the ominous significance of anyone other than the king adopting the royal regalia. Yet another
bad omen occurred while Alexander was making the final preparations for
his landforces' departure for Arabia. When the king momentarily left the
royal throne unoccupied, a prisoner made his way forward and sat down

A 3rd-century BCE
copy of a naked
marble torso
after Lysippus
respresenting
Alexander as Pan.

A FAREWELL FOR THE SOLDIERS

Arrian describes the accounts in the royal journal (see page 45) of Alexander's final hours: "... the soldiers were passionately eager to see him; some hoped for a sight of him while he was still alive; others wished to see his body, for a report had gone round that he was already dead, and they suspected, I fancy, that his death was being concealed by his guards. But nothing could keep them from a sight of him, and the motive in almost every heart was grief and a sort of helpless bewilderment at the thought of losing their king. Lying speechless as the men filed by, he yet struggled to raise his head, and in his eyes there was a look of recognition for each individual as he passed."

on it—a capital offence. The royal eunuchs were filled with terror, for this was also seen as a portent of disaster to come.

In spite of such ominous omens, by 29 May Alexander was ready for battle. He made sacrifices and appealed to the gods for success on his Arabian expedition, before distributing wine and gifts among the troops. In the evening the king attended a great feast in honor of his close friend Nearchus, who was to take command of the naval forces. After the banquet, Alexander went on to drink heavily with some of his Companions before retiring to bathe and sleep, as was his custom. The next evening the king once again drank heavily into the early hours, despite the onset of a fever. However, by 31 May the fever—perhaps caused by an infection or malaria—had grown more severe, and Alexander had to be transported on a litter in order to perform his daily sacrifices, although he was still instructing his senior officers regarding plans for the Arabian campaign, which he fully intended to lead himself.

As evening approached, it was decided to take the ailing king across the Euphrates to the cooler surroundings of the palace gardens, where he recovered enough to spend the next day talking freely with his colleagues and playing dice. The following morning, he discussed the forthcoming expedition with Nearchus. Yet, once again, the fever returned and began to take increasing effect on Alexander's battle-ravaged body, so much so that he was carried back to the palace with his senior officers in close attendance. By 7 June it was obvious that the king was very seriously ill. Alexander lost his powers of speech as his life-force slowly began to ebb away.

On the night of 9 June, desperately seeking the assistance of the gods, some of the royal Companions (including Attalus and Seleucus) spent the night in the temple of Bel. They asked the god whether Alexander should be brought into the temple to pray, to which Bel is said to have replied that it would be better for the king to remain undisturbed.

With the Macedonian officers gathered anxiously around his bedside, Alexander gave his royal ring to Perdiccas, officially appointing him acting deputy and Regent. It is said that, when he was asked to whom he left his empire, the king simply whispered *"hoti to kratisto"*—"to the best." Shortly afterward, on the evening of 10 June, Alexander the Great died. He was not quite 33 years old.

A 14th-century CE Mughal illustration depicts Roxane as a veiled figure lamenting over the body of Alexander, surrounded by his men.

THE STRUGGLE FOR SUCCESSION

J ust before he died, Alexander is said to have predicted that tremenrary funerary games would be played out after his death. However, even he could not have imagined the murderous rivalries his passing would unleash upon the ancient world. For more than 40 years, the empire Alexander had created and held together by sheer force of personality was ripped apart in his officers' violent power struggles. Yet, as events were to prove, none of them had the ability to control an empire that stretched from Macedonia in the west to India in the east, north to the Danube and south to the borders of Nubia.

In the days following Alexander's death, bewilderment must have given way to tremendous grief among his troops. As the king's body lay in the palace of Nebuchadnezzar, the Persians shaved their heads and tore at their garments in traditional gestures of mourning. When news of Alexander's demise reached the great dowager Persian queen Sisygambis, she simply refused all food and drink, and died five days later.

It has been suggested that when Alexander whispered that he left his empire "*hoti to kratisto*," ("to the best"), he may actually have spoken the name of Craterus (*Kratero*) rather than "*kratisto*." It is therefore possible that Alexander's last wishes were intentionally misunderstood by those who did not want Craterus as their leader. Craterus had always served jointly with Hephaestion as Alexander's second-in-command, and had already been appointed Regent of Macedon to replace the elderly Antipater. However, at the time of the king's death Craterus was still on his way back to Pella. The news reached him in Cilicia.

In Craterus' absence, Alexander had appointed Perdiccas to act for him by giving him the royal seal ring. "After Alexander's death, Perdiccas at once succeeded in concentrating the greatest power in his hands," writes Plutarch. Determined to keep the empire together, Perdiccas quickly turned his attention to the succession.

The Macedonian monarchy had never been a straightforward hereditary office, and there were numerous candidates who could claim royal status. Alexander had not named an heir and, although his widow Roxane was pregnant, there was no way of knowing the sex of her unborn child. Anxious to secure the future for Alexander's only legitimate offspring, Roxane acted swiftly to exterminate any potential rivals. Immediately after her husband's death, she summoned his second wife Stateira to Babylon. Stateira arrived with her sister Drypetis, Hephaestion's widow, as yet unaware that Alexander was dead. Darius' daughters shared their father's fate—Roxane murdered them and hid their bodies in a well.

According to Plutarch, Roxane's actions had the support of Perdiccas, and the two now joined forces. Perdiccas summoned the council of generals and proposed that they should await the birth of Roxane's child and, if male, proclaim him king. Many of the rank-and-file soldiers refused, saying that the king should be a pure Macedonian. The only possible alternative was Alexander's retarded half-brother Arrhidaeus (see page 15), now in his late-30s. It was eventually decided that Arrhidaeus should be made king, with Craterus to act as his guardian under Perdiccas' supervision, while everyone awaited the outcome of Roxane's pregnancy. When, in August 323BCE, she gave birth to a healthy boy—named Alexander after his father—a dual monarchy was proclaimed. As Alexander IV, the child was to rule jointly with his uncle, who would be known as Philip III.

Alexander the Great's death sparked rebellion among the Greek city-states. Led by Athens, they raised a force of allies and mercenaries together with a great fleet. Craterus crossed from Asia with sufficient troops to join Antipater in putting down the revolt. Antipater and Craterus then prepared

So convoluted and bloody was the fight for succession that, of all Alexander's generals, the only one to die in his bed was the king's rumored half-brother Ptolemy. The dynasty he founded would span three centuries.

This silver *tetradrachm* of Seleucus I, King of Syria, was minted at Persepolis ca. 300BCE. Seleucus, having survived years of hard campaigning under Alexander, enjoyed a taste of power but was eventually killed in the endless feuding between the Macedonian generals that followed the king's death.

to march against Perdiccas. Meanwhile, Ptolemy seized both Egypt—the wealthiest part of the empire—and Alexander's body (see page 158). Perdiccas marched into Egypt in 321BCE, but failed to regain control. His men mutinied and killed him.

Perdiccas' able deputy Eumenes successfully held back the invading forces of Antipater and Craterus at the Dardanelles, where Craterus was killed in action. Antipater appointed his friend Antigonus "the One-Eyed" as commander in Asia Minor and returned to Macedonia with the kings Philip and Alexander. For two years, Antipater ruled through them as regent until his death in 319BCE at the age of 79. After a power struggle with his father's general Polyperchon, Antipater's son Cassander persuaded King Philip to appoint him regent and went on to establish his hold over the whole of Greece.

Accompanied by the six-year-old Alexander IV and his mother Roxane, Polyperchon fled to Epirus, where the three joined forces with Olympias, still as formidable as ever. As soon as Olympias crossed over the border into Macedon with Polyperchon's troops, Philip's men deserted to her side. The unfortunate King Philip and his wife Eurydice were executed on her orders in 317BCE, making her grandson Alexander IV sole king. However, Olympias did not outlive her latest prey for long. Cassander ordered her execution in 316BCE; she met her death with great courage.

Cassander imprisoned the young king Alexander. His empire was now effectively controlled by five great powers (*diadochi*) independent of any central authority. Although Cassander controlled Macedonia and Greece, Ptolemy had established himself in Egypt, Lysimachus held Thrace, Seleucus controlled Syria, and Antigonus ruled Asia Minor. Yet more in-fighting followed, during which Ptolemy, Cassander, Lysimachus, and Seleucus were forced to unite against Antigonus. In 311BCE, when stalemate was reached, Cassander took the opportunity to remove the last remaining unifying factor by ordering the execution of the 13-year-old Alexander IV and his mother Roxane. With the death of Alexander the Great's only legitimate heir, each general went on to proclaim himself ruler of his respective area, and the empire divided into independent kingdoms.

Antigonus and his son Demetrius now attempted to take over the others' lands and re-establish the empire. Once Demetrius had invaded and liberated Athens, Antigonus sent him to attack and ultimately defeat Ptolemy's navy at Salamis. A failed invasion of Egypt followed in 306BCE. Ptolemy, Cassander, Lysimachus, and Seleucus once again united against Antigonus. Seleucus and Lysimachus finally met Antigonus and Demetrius at Ipsus in Phrygia in 301BCE. At the so-called "Battle of the Kings," Seleucus' 500 Indian war elephants proved decisive. Antigonus was killed in the battle, ending any chance of Alexander's empire ever being restored. Only four great power bases now remained, the separate kingdoms of the ruthless monarchs Ptolemy I of Egypt, Cassander of Greece, Seleucus I of Syria, and Lysimachus, who extended his Thracian territories to include western and central Asia Minor. Lysimachus was killed in 281BCE in a battle against Seleucus. When Seleucus then attempted to claim Lysimachus' kingdom he in turn was assassinated.

Detail of the reliefs on the walls of the barque shrine of Amun in Karnak temple, Egypt. Alexander's successor Philip III Arrhidaeus (323–317BCE) is shown being crowned and presented to the gods in their enclosed barques.

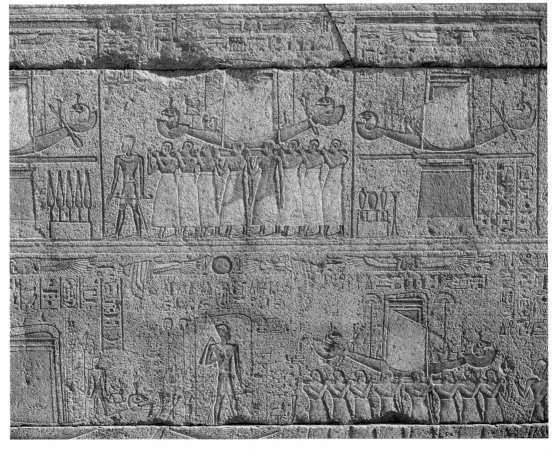

THE LOST TOMB

Following Alexander's death, the regent Perdiccas decided to keep the king's body—an important symbol of power—in Babylon until he felt the empire was secure, before sending it to Aegae, the Macedonian capital, for burial. Alexander's embalmed body lay in state in full view of the many thousands who wished to pay tribute while work went ahead on all the spectacular trappings that would accompany it to its final resting place. Craftsmen from across the empire produced funerary equipment of unsurpassed expense and beauty. The preserved body, embedded in spices, was then placed within a jeweled sarcophagus of beaten gold. Over it was spread a purple funerary pall embroidered with gold, on top of which lay Alexander's armor and Trojan shield. Around this was erected a magnificent golden shrine.

The great funeral cortege set out on its slow, stately progress in 321BCE. Sixty-four mules were to draw the whole catafalque the thousands of miles from Babylon to Aegae. Diodorus, taking his information from an eye-witness account, states that the famous procession "drew many spectators. From every city it came to, people came out to meet it and accompany it when it went on its way, never wearying of their pleasure in the sight."

However, Alexander's body never reached his homeland. As the cortege approached Syria, Ptolemy seized it and took it back to Egypt, where, he insisted, Alexander had wanted to be buried, close to his father Amun. This act established Ptolemy as Alexander's successor in Egypt; he went on to proclaim himself Pharaoh in 306BCE (see page 157). Ptolemy ordered the construction of an Egyptian-style tomb for Alexander in Memphis. Meanwhile, work began on a mausoleum in Alexandria, the coastal city Alexander had founded in 331BCE. After Ptolemy I's death in

293BCE, his son Ptolemy II Phiadelphus (293–246BCE) finally laid Alexander's body to rest in an elaborate marble mausoleum in the city. The body lay on public display in its gold coffin until 89BCE, when Ptolemy IX melted down the sarcophagus to produce coinage. Outraged, the people of Alexandria re-interred Alexander in a glass sarcophagus. The last of the Ptolemies, Cleopatra VII, visited the tomb with Julius Caesar in 45BCE. Several Roman emperors also came to pay their respects—the last reported imperial visitor was Caracalla in 215BCE. It has been suggested that Alexander's tomb may have been destroyed during urban riots in the reign of Aurelian (270–275CE). By the fourth century CE the tomb's whereabouts had become obscured—today it is lost.

The entrance to the mosque of Nabi Daniel in Alexandria. This is reputed by some to be built on the site of Alexander's lost tomb.

Underwater archeological research has recently begun to reveal the Ptolemaic city. Based on the writings of Strabo, excavations on land by those searching for the lost tomb have closed in on a cemetery site featuring alabaster walls, floors, and ceiling. Alexander the Great may yet lie somewhere beneath the streets of modern Alexandria awaiting rediscovery.

THE EMPEROR AND THE CONQUEROR'S TOMB

Three hundred years after Alexander's death, Augustus, the founder of the Roman empire, traveled to Alexandria to visit the great king's tomb:

"About this time he had the sarcophagus containing Alexander the Great's mummy removed from the Mausoleum at Alexandria, and after a long look at its features, showed his veneration by crowning the head with a golden diadem and strewing flowers on the trunk. When asked, 'Would you now like to visit the Mausoleum of the Ptolemies?' he replied, 'I came to see a King, not a row of corpses.'"

Suetonius, *The Twelve Caesars*, 18.1

THE LEGACY
OF ALEXANDER

An 18th-century sculpture depicts two mourners outside Alexander's tent. Even years after the king's death, his generals still felt the need for his presence: in 318BCE, they met to discuss their differences in Alexander's own tent, before his royal scepter, his robes, and his empty throne.

Although many aspects of the cross-cultural world Alexander had created either died with him or were destroyed in the long conflicts that followed his death, he had nevertheless changed the ancient world irrevocably. He carried classical culture to the foothills of the Himalaya, founded more than seventy cities, and revolutionized international trade.

Alexander's reign marked the end of the Classical era and the dawn of the Hellenistic age, which was to last for three hundred years. When Alexander ascended the throne, the idea of a Greek monarchy had become largely restricted to Macedonia. His successors created a series of Greek monarchies which controlled the area of his former empire between mainland Greece and Afghanistan, founding their own dynasties in true Macedonian style. He became the prototype for the kings of the Hellenistic world, who, like him, were worshiped by their people.

By 275BCE, after almost 50 years of conflict in the wake of Alexander's death (see pages 154–7), three major dynastic kingdoms had emerged, ruled by the Seleucids, the Ptolemies (see box, opposite), and the Antigonids. The Seleucid kings controlled by far the largest landmass. Even after

A DYNASTY OF GREEK PHARAOHS

The Ptolemies were without question the most tenacious of Alexander's successors. While the kingdoms of their rivals were absorbed one-by-one into Rome's expanding empire, the often murderous Ptolemaic kings managed to retain control of Egypt for three centuries. They spent the fabulous wealth generated by trade through their capital, Alexandria, on vast building projects, including the restoration of ancient pharaonic temples and the construction of grand Greek-style buildings in the royal city. The Ptolemies also made their capital the world center for scholarship and the arts by creating a state-funded university with a remarkable associated Great Library.

If Ptolemy I had indeed been Alexander's half-brother, then Cleopatra VII—the last Ptolemaic pharaoh—must also have been a descendant of the Macedonian king. Perhaps inspired by her illustrious ancestor, Cleopatra almost managed to resurrect Egypt's ancient empire. When, in 30BCE, the queen committed suicide rather than submit to the subjugation of Rome, her death marked the end of the Hellenistic age that had begun with the death of Alexander himself.

Seleucus I ceded his Indian territory to the Indian king Chandragupta Maurya in exchange for 500 elephants in 302BCE, the Seleucid kingdom stretched from Syria to Afghanistan and contained around 30 million people. As well as Egypt and its seven million inhabitants, the Ptolemies controlled parts of Libya, southern Syria, Cyprus, and the Aegean islands, while the Antigonids of Macedonia ruled over approximately four million subjects.

Many of the towns and cities Alexander had founded continued to flourish in the centuries after his death. These outposts of Greek culture, scattered across the East from Egypt to Tadzhikistan, shared a common Greek language, permanently marking out the areas of Alexander's conquests. Greek settlers, who often colonized previously uninhabited areas, brought great prosperity to these regions. The Seleucids themselves founded some 60 settlements between western Turkey and Iran, from their joint capitals Antioch in Syria and Seleucia-on-the-Tigris near Babylon to the Persian city of Susa, which they renamed Seleucia-on-the-Eulaeus. The Ptolemies poured their energies into the Egyptian Alexandria and made it their capital—it eventually become the greatest city of the ancient world in terms of trade, culture, and wealth. However, Alexander's successors effectively overturned his policy of blending Greek and native practices wherever he had felt it appropriate. The local customs and traditions Alexander had tried to amalgamate with the Greek lifestyle were now largely subsumed by an imposed Greek culture. This resulted in kingdoms dominated by a Greek élite ruling over a "barbarian" native population (although the extent to which these non-Greeks then adopted Greek practices remains the subject of continuing debate among scholars).

Nevertheless, the mixed populations of these numerous cities enjoyed many of the benefits of Greek civilization that Alexander had originally brought to the east, from defensive walls capable of withstanding ever more sophisticated siege equipment to increasingly efficient systems of communication. The towns' Greek political constitutions were largely based on democratic principles, with magistrates, councils, and popular assemblies. Civic architecture incorporated standard Greek features, such as grand administrative buildings, temples, libraries, theaters, and gymnasia.

Greek culture was thus exported to every corner of Alexander's empire. By the mid-third century BCE, for example, the Greek settlement of Ai Khanoum in Bactria (modern Afghanistan) boasted a library well

HAD HE LIVED

Plutarch states that in the months before his death, Alexander "spent his time with his engineers and architects planning projects which were even more outlandish and extravagant" than those he had already realized. On the eternal question of what Alexander might have gone on to do, had he not died so young, Arrian writes:

"Personally I have no data from which to infer precisely what Alexander had in mind, and I do not care to make guesses; one thing, however, I feel I can say without fear of contradiction, and that is that his plans, whatever they were, had no lack of grandeur or ambition: he would never have remained idle in the enjoyment of any of his conquests, even had he extended his empire from Asia to Europe and from Europe to the British Isles. On the contrary, he would have continued to seek beyond them for unknown lands, as it was ever his nature, if he had no rival, to strive to better his own best."

stocked with philosophical teachings written on papyrus rolls, a great theater with seating for 5,000, and an administrative center of regal proportions, its buildings embellished with finely crafted architectural features and beautiful mosaic floors to rival any found in mainland Greece. The inhabitants of Ai Khanoum chose to adorn a shrine in their gymnasium building with an inscription copied from the temple of Delphi some 3,000 miles away in Greece. The inscriptions are referred to as the "wise words of famous men of old, consecrated in holy Delphi from where Clearchus took them, copying them carefully to set them shining from afar in the sacred enclosure of Cineas," the Thessalian founder of the city.

A terracotta 1st-century BCE medallion featuring the head of Alexander as the sun god Helios, his hair splayed out to resemble the rays of the sun.

Elsewhere in Bactria, at the Greek settlement of Kandahar, the beliefs of the Indian king and Buddhist convert Asoka (ca. 268–232BCE), grandson of Chandragupta Maurya, were expressed in sophisticated Greek terms, displaying a thorough knowledge of Greek philosophy. Dated to ca. 257BCE, Asoka's Kandahar inscription also includes a list of his fellow kings from his Asian borders right across to Egypt. There, further bilingual and trilingual inscriptions composed of both Greek and Egyptian texts have been found, including the famous Rosetta Stone—the means by which Egyptian hieroglyphs were finally translated at the beginning of the 19th century CE.

A shared Greek language was not the only means by which Alexander unified his empire—through his establishment and development of new communication networks he had an enormous impact on the economy of the ancient world. He transformed a series of individual, isolated regions—the economies of which were based largely on a system of exchange and barter—into a vast single market in which traders used the millions of standard coins produced in Alexander's mints (see page 68), and later in those of his successors. Alexander's program of establishing

The story of Alexander inspired many artists down the ages. *Alexander's Entry into Babylon* was painted by the French artist Charles Le Brun (1619–1690) during the reign of Louis XIV. The French king regarded the Macedonian leader as a role model, as did many of the great monarchs of Europe, including the later emperor Napoleon I Bonaparte (1769–1821).

cities in locations with great trading potential was also to have a lasting impact on the world market. The ultimate example of this was the Egyptian Alexandria. By founding the city on the Mediterranean coast, Alexander successfully opened up Egypt to outside trade and influence, resulting in drastic changes to its ancient, conservative culture. Alexandria went on to become the most important marketplace in the ancient world.

The new routes of communication Alexander opened up across both land and sea during the course of his campaigns were exploited through his establishment of coastal settlements equiped with harbors large enough to house a fleet. There followed an explosion in international trade. Suddenly, goods, people, and armies could move around an area stretching from northern Europe to the Indian subcontinent and as far as China. New trade routes sprang up and were busy with traders and craftsmen, bureaucrats and government officials, and the sportsmen and performers who journeyed between Greek-style competitions. Scholars traveled between the many new Hellenistic centers of learning. Pilgrims journeyed to one of any number of shrines holy to the Greeks or Egyptians, Persians, or Indians—Asoka's Buddhist missionary monks, for example, carried their message all the way from India to Syria.

Amazed at the enormous changes wrought by Alexander's campaigns, people of every era have wondered what the great conqueror would have gone on to achieve had he not died so young (see also box, page 162). What impact might further conquests have had on the world? Alexander left ambitious plans. He had intended to build magnificent temples in honor of his favorite gods. In addition to the costly restoration of the temple of Bel in Babylon, he wanted to create a huge new complex for Athena at Troy, and had allocated some 10,000 talents to build temples across Greece. At the time of his death, the king had been working on plans for his memorial to Hephaestion, a huge pyramid-like ziggurat costing an estimated 12,000 talents. He also intended to build a tomb for his father Philip, "which should be like the greatest pyramids of Egypt." However, in the uncertainty that characterizes the aftermath of a king's death, his successors decided not to carry out any of these projects—they were simply too ambitious and too expensive.

Alexander's future plans were not limited to building works. Just before he died, he had been planning the creation of yet more Greek settlements deep in the Persian heartlands in Persis and Media. Following his imminent Arabian campaign, he also intended to found trading settlements along the coast of Arabia, creating a new trade area to rival Phoenicia. In 322BCE, joined by Antipater and the new Macedonian recruits, it seems that Alexander was planning to begin his westward expansion, marching along the North African coast past Carthage as far as the Straits of Gibraltar. From there he would surely have led his army into Spain and beyond into the limitless unknown.

Already a legend during his lifetime, Alexander's premature death at the age of 32 saw his mythical status take on epic proportions. Five hundred years later the "Romance of Alexander"—a collection of tales published in Alexandria—was an international bestseller, translated from the original Greek into many languages, including Latin, Hebrew, and Arabic. The Macedonian king who conquered the known world continued to inspire individuals throughout history, from the successors who sought to emulate him to such diverse figures as Julius Caesar, Cleopatra, Augustus, Louis XIV, and Napoleon, all of whom dreamed of following where Alexander had first led.

ALEXANDER'S PEOPLE

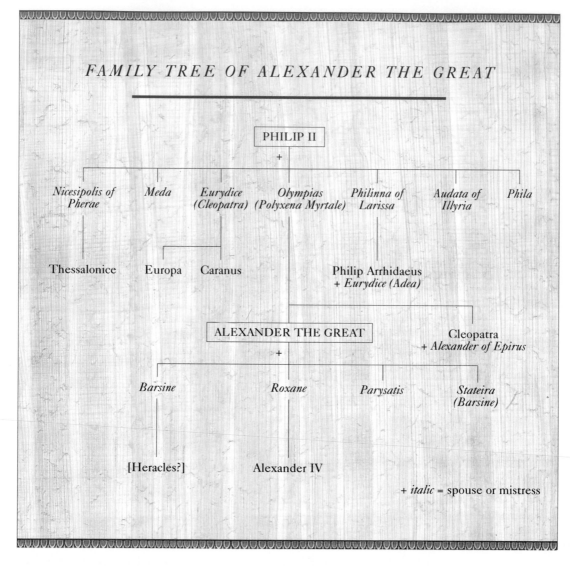

FAMILY TREE OF ALEXANDER THE GREAT

PHILIP II
+

Nicesipolis of Pherae — Meda — *Eurydice (Cleopatra)* — *Olympias (Polyxena Myrtale)* — *Philinna of Larissa* — *Audata of Illyria* — *Phila*

Thessalonice — Europa — Caranus — Philip Arrhidaeus + *Eurydice (Adea)*

ALEXANDER THE GREAT
+

Cleopatra + *Alexander of Epirus*

Barsine — *Roxane* — *Parysatis* — *Stateira (Barsine)*

[Heracles?] — Alexander IV

+ *italic* = spouse or mistress

Ada Queen of Caria; returned to her throne by Alexander, whom she adopted as her son

Alexander King of Epirus and brother of Olympias

Alexander III King of Macedon 336–323BCE

Antigonus Monophthalmus "the one-eyed" Governor of Phrygia; ruler of Asia Minor after Alexander's death

Antipater Alexander's deputy and regent of Macedon

Ariobarzanes Persian general and governor

Aristander Army seer

Aristobulos of Phocis Engineer, served with Alexander; author of a history of Alexander's campaigns

Aristotle Philosopher and tutor to young Alexander

Arrian of Nicomedeia Greek historian; author of a 2nd-century CE history of Alexander

Artabazus Rebel Persian nobleman and friend of Philip II; ally of Alexander

Arybbas King of Epirus

Attalus Companion under Philip II

Bagoas Eunuch and attendant of Darius III; Alexander's lover

Barsine Possible mistress of Alexander and supposed mother of their son Heracles

Bessus Persian governor of Bactria; cousin of Darius III

Callisthenes Philosopher; nephew of Aristotle; Alexander's official campaign historian

Campaspe Greek mistress of Alexander

Caranus Philip II's son by Eurydice, killed in infancy

Cassander Son of Antipater

Chandragupta Maurya Founder of the first Indian empire

Chares Alexander's chamberlain; author of an account of life at court

Cleitus Known as "Black Cleitus"; commander of the royal squadron of the Companion Cavalry

Cleopatra Daughter of Philip II and Olympias; sister of Alexander

Cleopatra VII Descendant of Ptolemy I and last Ptolemaic pharaoh of Egypt

Coenus General; phalanx commander

Craterus General; second-incommand after the death of Parmenio

Darius III Born Codomannus, last Great King of Persia 336–330BCE

Demosthenes Anti-Macedonian Athenian orator

Diodorus Siculus 1st-century CE Greek historian

Drypetis Second daughter of Darius III; wife of Hephaestion

Eumenes of Cardia Alexander's chief private secretary

Eurydice Niece of Attalus; born Cleopatra; wife of Philip II

Harpalus Royal treasurer

Hephaestion Alexander's childhood friend and lifelong companion

Heracles Possible illegitimate son of Alexander by Barsine

Lanice Nurse to Alexander as a child; sister of Cleitus

Leonidas Kinsman of Olympias; responsible for Alexander's early education

Lysimachus Acarnanian courtier; supervised Alexander's early military training

Lysimachus King of Thrace after Alexander's death

Lysippus Alexander's sculptor

Mazaces Persian governor of Egypt, retained under Alexander's administration

Mazaeus Persian governor of Babylon

Nabarzanes Cavalry general and commander of Persian guard under Darius III

Nearchus Satrap of Lydia; later batallion commander of the guards and admiral of the fleet

Olympias Born Polyxena Myrtale, Epirot princess; wife of Philip II; mother of Alexander the Great

Omphis (Ambhi) Also known by his dynastic title of Taxiles, king of Taxila in India; ally of Alexander

Onesicritus of Cos Steersman of the fleet

Oxathres Brother of Darius III

Oxyartes Bactrian nobleman; father of Roxane

Parmenio General under Philip II and Alexander; father-inlaw of Attalus; father of Philotas

Parysatis Persian princess; wife of Alexander

Perdiccas Leading commander and friend of Alexander; acted as regent after the king's death

Philip Arrhidaeus Son of Philip II and Philinna of Larissa; elder half-brother of Alexander; ruled jointly with Alexander IV as Philip III after Alexander III's death

Philip II of Macedon King of Macedon; father of Alexander the Great

Philotas Son of Parmenio; Companion cavalry commander

Plutarch of Chaeronea 1st–2nd century CE historian; author of a life of Alexander

Porus Indian king; defeated and reinstated by Alexander

Ptolemy Friend and rumored half-brother of Alexander; pharaoh of Egypt (305–283BCE) after Alexander's death; founder of Ptolemaic dynasty; author of a lost history of Alexander

Roxane Bactrian noblewoman; wife of Alexander and mother of his posthumous son and successor Alexander IV

Satibarzanes Persian governor of Aria

Seleucus Companion; founder of Seleucid dynasty after Alexander's death

Sisygambis Mother of Darius III of Persia

Spitamenes Sogdian nobleman

Stateira Originally called Barsine, eldest daughter of Darius III; wife of Alexander

GLOSSARY

Achaemenid empire Persian empire founded in 548BCE by Cyrus the Great and defeated by Alexander.

Achilles Greek hero of Homer's *Iliad*. Alexander claimed Achilles as an ancestor.

Ahura Mazda Principal Persian deity, the god of light.

Amun (Libyan Ammon) Egyptian god whom Alexander equated with the Greek king of the gods, Zeus.

Anti-Macedonian League Formed by the Greek city-states, led by Athens, as a defense against Macedonian expansion under Philip II.

Argead dynasty Macedonian royal dynasty founded in the 7th century BCE by Argaios.

barbarian Derogative Greek term used to denote all non-Greeks, including Persians.

city-state Greek state consisting of a sovereign city and its dependencies.

Companions (*Hetairoi*) Macedonian élite, made up of male members of aristocratic households.

Dionysus Greek god of wine and revelry, also worshiped as the personification of the life-force.

Endless Ocean Sea the Greeks believed encircled the world.

Great King (King of Kings) Persian monarch and ruler of the Achaemenid empire.

Hellenistic age (323–30BCE) Period lasting from Alexander's death until the death of Cleopatra VII of Egypt, during which a series of Greek monarchies controlled the area of Alexander's former empire.

Helios Sun god.

Hellenic League League of the Greek city-states (except Sparta) formed by Philip II.

Heracles Greek demi-god and son of Zeus.

kyrbasia Persian cap, which the Great King wore in royal fashion with the point erect.

phalanx (meaning "finger") Macedonian military formation made up of 4,096 pikemen armed with *sarissa*s.

Pharaoh King of Egypt, a Greek term derived from the Egyptian *per-aa* ("Great House").

Prometheus Greek demi-god and hero.

proskynesis Greek term describing respectful Persian gestures, including the ceremonial prostration.

Ptolemaic dynasty Dynasty of Greek kings of Egypt, founded by Ptolemy I, who proclaimed himself Pharaoh in 306BCE. The last Ptolemaic ruler was Queen Cleopatra VII, who died in 30BCE.

"Romance of Alexander" A collection of tales about Alexander published in Alexandria 500 years after the king's death.

sarissa Long, cornel-wood pike tipped with an iron blade; the weapon of the Macedonian phalanx.

satrap Governor appointed by the Persian king to rule over a region of the Persian empire.

talent Unit of ancient Greek coinage, worth 6,000 *drachmae*.

Zeus Supreme Greek deity, king of the gods. Olympias told the young Alexander that Zeus (whom Alexander later equated with the Egyptian god Amun), rather than Philip II, was his father.

FURTHER READING

Boardman, J., Griffin, J., and Murray, O., eds. *The Oxford History of the Classical World*. Oxford University Press: Oxford, 1991.

Bowman, A.K. *Egypt After the Pharaohs 332 BC–AD 642*. British Museum Press: London, 1986.

Briant, P. *De la Grèce à l'Orient: Alexandre le Grand*. Découvertes Gallimard: Paris, 1987.

Burn, A.R. *The Pelican History of Greece*. Pelican: Harmondsworth, 1974.

Bury, J.B. and Meiggs, R. *A History of Greece to the Death of Alexander the Great*. Macmillan: London, 1983.

Cawkwell, G. *Philip of Macedon*. Heinemann Educational Books: London, 1981.

Cotterell, A., ed. *The Penguin Encyclopedia of Ancient Civilizations*. Penguin: Harmondsworth, 1980.

Davies, J.K. *Democracy and the Classical World*. Fontana: London, 1984.

Empereur, J. *Alexandria Rediscovered*. British Museum Press: London, 1998.

Forster, E.M. *Alexandria: a History and Guide*. Michael Haag Ltd.: London, 1982.

Fraser, P.M. *Ptolemaic Alexandria*. Oxford University Press: Oxford, 1972.

Grant, Michael *From Alexander to Cleopatra: the Hellenistic World*. Weidenfeld and Nicolson: London, 1982.

Green, P. *Alexander the Great*. Weidenfeld and Nicolson: London, 1973.

Hammond, N.G.L. *Alexander the Great: King, Commander and Statesman*. The Bristol Press: Bristol, 1989.

Holbl, G. *A History of the Ptolemaic Empire*. Routledge: London, 2001.

Humble, R. *Warfare in the Ancient World*. Cassell: London, 1980.

Kitto, H.D.F *The Greeks*. Pelican: Harmondsworth, 1979.

Lane Fox, R. *Alexander the Great*. Penguin: Harmondsworth, 1973.

Levi, P. *Atlas of the Greek World*. Phaidon: Oxford, 1980.

Lewis, N. *Greeks in Ptolemaic Egypt*. Clarendon Press: Oxford, 1986.

Lloyd, J.G. *Alexander the Great: Selections from Arrian*. Cambridge University Press: Cambridge, 1981.

Luce, J.V. *Homer and the Heroic Age*. Futura: London, 1979.

Mahaffy, J.P. *A History of Egypt IV: the Ptolemaic Dynasty*. Methuen & Co.: London, 1899.

Milton, J. *Sunrise of Power: Alexander and the World of Hellenism*. Boston Publishing Company: Boston, 1986.

Plutarch (trans. I.Scott-Kilvert) *The Age of Alexander: Nine Greek Lives by Plutarch*. Penguin: Harmondsworth, 1973.

Pomeroy, S.B. *Goddesses, Whores, Wives and Slaves: Women in Classical Antiquity*. Schocken Books: New York, 1975.

Prag, J. and Neave, R. *Making Faces: using forensic and archaeological evidence*. British Museum Press: London, 1997.

Prag, A.J.N.W. "Reconstructing King Philip II," *American Journal of Archaeology* 94, pp.237–247, 1990.

Prag, A.J.N.W., Musgrave, J.H., and Neave, R.A.H. "The Skull from Tomb II at Vergina: King Philip II of Macedon," *Journal of Hellenic Studies* 104, pp.60–78, 1984.

Renault, M. *The Nature of Alexander*. Allen Lane: London, 1975.

la Riche, W. *Alexandria, the Sunken City*. Weidenfeld and Nicolson: London, 1996.

Schreider, H. and Schreider, F. "In the Footsteps of Alexander the Great," *National Geographic*, 133 (1), pp.1–66, 1968.

True, M., and Hamma, K., eds. *Alexandria and Alexandrianism*. Getty Museum: Malibu, 1996.

Walbank, F.W. *The Hellenistic World*. Fontana: London, 1981.

Wheeler, M. *Flames Over Persepolis: Turning Point in History*. Weidenfeld and Nicolson: London, 1968.

INDEX

ACKNOWLEDGMENTS

PUBLISHERS' ACKNOWLEDGMENTS

The publishers would like to thank the following people, museums, and photographic libraries for kind permission to reproduce their material. Every care has been taken to trace copyright holders. However, if we have omitted anyone we apologize and will, if informed, make corrections in any future edition.

Picture credits:

Key
BAL   Bridgeman Art Library, London/New York
BM   British Museum, London
AA   Art Archive, London
NGIC   National Geographic Image Collection
RHPL   Robert Harding Picture Library

Front cover: AKG/Archaeological Museum, Istanbul; **1** BM (GR839); **2** AA/Staatliche Glytothek/Dagli Orti; **6** AKG/Archaeological Museum, Istanbul; **11** NGIC/James L. Stansfield; **12–13** Corbis/Gianni Dagli Orti; **15** AA/Chiaramonti Museum, Vatican/Dagli Orti; **16** AA/Archaeological Museum, Thessaloniki; **17** BAL/Fitzwilliam Museum, Cambridge; **18** AKG/Archaeological Museum, Istanbul; **19** AA/Pella Museum/Dagli Orti; **20** AA; **21** AKG; **22** BM (B210); **25** NGIC/James L. Stansfield; **27** RHPL; **29** AKG/Kunsthistorisches Museum, Vienna; **31t** Corbis/Sheldan Collins; **31b** BAL/Kunsthistorisches Museum, Vienna; **32** Corbis/Gianni Dagli Orti; **33** BAL/Archaeological Museum, Thessaloniki; **34** AKG; **37** BAL/Private Collection; **38** AKG; **40** AKG/Archaeological Museum, Istanbul; **41** RHPL; **42** Alinari; **44** RHPL; **47** Scala; **48–9** AKG/National Museum of Archaeology, Naples; **51** BM (GR869); **53** BAL; **54** AA&A; **55** AA&A; **57** Corbis/Yann Arthus-Bertrand; **58** BM (1919-8-20-1); **61** RHPL; **62–3** BAL/Louvre; **64** AKG/National Museum of Archaeology, Naples; **67** Corbis/Nik Wheeler; **68** BAL/Fitzwilliam Museum,

Cambridge; **69** BAL/Louvre; **70** AA/Dagli Orti; **71** Michael Holford/BM; **72** RHPL; **73** RHPL; **75** Corbis/K.M. Westermann; **76–7** RHPL; **79** Corbis/Gianni Dagli Orti; **81** BAL/Royal Asiatic Society; **83** AA/Archaeological Museum, Thessaloniki/Dagli Orti; **84** BM; **85** AA; **89** Axiom/Chris Caldicott; **91** BM (WAA124081); **93** BL (Or12208 f.312); **94** Novosti Agency; **95** BL (Or284 f.274v); **96** AA/Museo del Prado, Madrid/Dagli Orti; **99** RHPL; **100–101** AKG/Erich Lessing; **103** RHPL/Nigel Blythe; **104** BM (GR1736); **107** RMN/Louvre/Herve Lanwandowski; **108** BAL/Pinacoteca Palazzo Conservatori, Rome; **109** AA/Dagli Orti; **111** Corbis/Ric Ergenbright; **112** AA/BM; **113** AA/Bibliotek Municiale, Reims/Dagli Orti; **114** BAL/Ashmolean Museum, Oxford; **115** BAL/BM; **116** BM (WAA123910); **118** AKG/Louvre; **119** Axiom/Giles Caldicott; **121** BL; **122** AKG/Musee Guimet; **125** RHPL; **126–7** RHPL; **129** AA/Siritide Museum, Policoro/Dagli Orti; **131** AA/Mechitarista Congregation, Venice/Dagli Orti; **132** BAL/BM; **134–5** NGIC/James L. Stansfield; **137** AA/Dagli Orti; **138** AKG/Louvre; **139** RHPL; **140** AKG/National Maritime Museum, Haifa; **144** AKG/Erich Lessing; **146** RHPL; **147** AKG/Louvre; **148** RHPL/Adam Woolfit; **151** AA/Pella Museum/Dagli Orti; **153** BAL; **155** Ny Carlsberg Glyptotek, Copenhagen; **156** BM; **157** AA/Dagli Orti; **159** Joann Fletcher; **160** Corbis/Araldo de Luca; **163** AA/Museo Civico, Trieste; **164–5** AA/Louvre/Dagli Orti.

Text permissions:

The publishers would like to thank the following for kind permission to reproduce the translations and copyright material in this book. Every care has been taken to trace copyright holders. However, if we have omitted anyone we apologize and will, if informed, make corrections in any future edition.

The Campaigns of Alexander by Arrian, translated by Aubrey de Sélincourt, revised by J.R. Hamilton (Penguin Classics, 1958, Revised edition 1971) copyright © Aubrey de Sélincourt, 1958;

The Age of Alexander: Nine Greek Lives by Plutarch, (translated by Ian Scott-Kilvert (Penguin Classics, 1973) copyright © Ian Scott-Kilvert, 1973; Alexander the Great by Robin Lane Fox (Allen Lane, 1973). Reproduced with permission of Curtis Brown Ltd., London, on behalf of Robin Lane Fox. Copyright © Robin Lane Fox; *The Twelve Caesars* by Suetonius, translated by Robert Graves, revised by Michael Grant (Penguin Classics, 1957, Second revised edition 1979). Translation copyright © Robert Graves, 1957. Revised edition copyright © Michael Grant Publications Ltd., 1979. Reproduced by permission of A.P. Watt Ltd. on behalf of the Robert Graves Copyright Trust.

AUTHORS' ACKNOWLEDGMENTS

Both authors benefited enormously from corroboration with leading scholars in the field, to whom they are very grateful. In 1980 Alan Fildes spent a great deal of time with the late Professor Manolis Andronicos as he was excavating the tomb of Philip II, discussing at length his work at the Royal Tombs of Macedonia and sharing the amazing discoveries he had recently made. The authors would like to thank Professor Fawzi el-Fakharani, Emeritus Professor of Graeco-Roman Archaeology at Alexandria University, who kindly discussed his excavations at Alexandria's ancient necropolis. Professor el-Fakharani was once a student of the late Sir Mortimer Wheeler, whose own excavations across Persia and India provided much of our knowledge regarding Alexander's eastern conquests.

Both authors are also grateful to Dr. John Prag of Manchester Museum, who led the team working alongside Professor Andronicos to recreate the face of Philip II from the remains found in his tomb. We have been greatly helped by discussions with colleagues, including military expert Sharon McDermott of Manchester University and Dr. Sandra Knudsen, Curator of Ancient Art at the Toledo Museum of Art, all of whom so generously shared their knowledge with us.